ANCIENT OCHRES

The Aboriginal Rock Paintings
of Mount Borradaile

DAVID ANDREW ROBERTS AND ADRIAN PARKER

 J.B. BOOKS AUSTRALIA

ANCIENT OCHRES
Published in 2003 by
J.B. Books Pty Ltd
PO Box 118, Marleston, South Australia 5033
Ph: (08) 8351 1688

The National Library of Australia Cataloguing-in-Publication data:-
Parker, Adrian, 1968-.
Roberts, David Andrew, 1969-.
Ancient ochres: the aboriginal rock paintings of Mount Borradaile.

Bibliography.
Includes index.
ISBN 1 876622 42 3.

1. Rock paintings — Northern Territory — Borradaile, Mount, Region. 2. Aborigines, Australian — Northern Territory — Borradaile, Mount, Region — Art.

709.01130994295

Design: Julianne Hare, LJ Design
Production: Victoria Jefferys, WriteLight Pty Ltd
Produced in Hong Kong through Phoenix Offset.

This book is respectfully dedicated to Max and Philippa Davidson, and to the traditional owners of Mount Borradaile, whose encouragement, hospitality and kindness have made it possible.

CONTENTS

FOREWORD

The Mount Borradaile region in northern Arnhem Land in the 'Top End' of the Northern Territory contains some of the most stunning rock paintings, not just in Australia but in the whole world. In terms of artistic quality, quantity, colourfulness and excellent state of preservation, this body of rock art is unrivalled. The walls of hundreds of rock-shelters are decorated with innumerable pictures documenting traditional Aboriginal life over many thousands of years. Subjects range from now-extinct animals to twentieth century sailing ships, and art techniques are equally varied, including stencils and the rare use of beeswax to portray the eyes and other features of some figures. As in much of Australian Aboriginal art, the largest and most elaborate paintings with finely drawn internal decoration portray Ancestral Beings from the Dreaming, the era of Creation. Such sites are of significance to Aboriginal traditional owners, who still recount stories describing the travels of the Rainbow Serpent and other Creative Ancestors across the landscape.

In view of the richness of the rock art and sheer natural beauty of Mount Borradaile, it is remarkable that this is the first book to be devoted to this particular region. In many ways, it has been a well-kept secret, in contrast with the much better known Kakadu National Park to its south. The Mt Borradaile region is Aboriginal land

and there is no public access, but in the 1980s, with the blessing of Aboriginal traditional owners, Max and Philippa Davidson set up a safari camp and air-strip there. Small groups of visitors fly in from Darwin or Jabiru to fish, bird-watch or to be guided to some of the major rock art galleries. The emphasis is on conservation of the cultural and natural environment. Mt Borradaile is not subjected to the drastic annual burning practised by the managers of Kakadu National Park and consequently one sees a much richer and more varied flora and fauna. Whether one wants to visit Australia's finest rock paintings, get close to crocodiles, watch brolgas dance or simply wander through a superb pristine wilderness, this is the place. The few days I spent at the multi-award winning Davidson's Arnhem Land Safaris were among the most memorable of my three decades involved in research and conservation of Australia's Aboriginal heritage.

Rock paintings are deteriorating rapidly due to natural factors such as erosion. Traditionally they were regularly touched-up or re-painted during annual ceremonies, but Aboriginal rock painting has now ceased. Sadly, this means that in fifty years time little will remain of the colourful paintings one sees at present. In this situation a first-class photographic archive is vital, which is one service provided by this book's authors, David Roberts and Adrian Parker. Yet *Ancient Ochres. The Aboriginal Rock Paintings of Mount Borradaile* is far more than a beautiful pictorial record or catalogue. Early chapters are devoted to a wide-ranging discussion of the land, its people and their history and the art, meaning and role of rock painting in the Mt Borradaile area and Arnhem Land as a whole. The book will enhance the experience of visitors to the region, provide a fascinating read for armchair travellers and scholars and serve as a valuable, permanent record of these fabulous paintings for both the descendants of the artists and the world at large.

Josephine Flood

INTRODUCTION

In 1875, the explorer John Lewis, on the plains near the head of the East Alligator River, commented on the `numbers of old castle-like rocks, some with native paintings on them, and many parcels and packets of bones we found in the melaleuca bark'. It was, though crude and unenthusiastic, among the first reports of the ancient landscape and art of the East Alligator River region.

A century later, a former buffalo shooter, Max Davidson, at home among the same castle-like rocks and melaleucas, located some of the world's most spectacular and intense rock art galleries. Even in a region famous for its surviving Aboriginal cultures and their ancient painting traditions, the sites found by Max are especially notable for their abundance, splendor and diversity.

Mount Borradaile — or Awunbarna — is one of the larger sandstone formations that tower above the vast expanse of coastal plain around Cooper Creek in the 'Top End' of Australia's Northern Territory. This region lies on the western edge of the Arnhem Land Aboriginal Reserve, adjacent to the World Heritage Kakadu National Park, and is traditionally owned by Aboriginal clansmen under the Aboriginal Land Rights (Northern Territory) Act of 1976. Mount Borradaile itself contains shelters and

A silent sentinel. Mount Borradaile overlooks the Cooper Creek floodplains. The immense outlier contains an amalgamation of habitation, art and burial sites which have been formally classified under the Northern Territory's Aboriginal Sacred Sites Act (1978).

sites of enormous importance, formally classified under the Northern Territory's Aboriginal Sacred Sites Act (1978).

For much of the estimated 55,000 years of human occupation of this area, the inhabitants recorded their presence in ochre on rock; one of their most important and durable mediums for describing life, law and history. It was a tradition that ceased in this area only 50 years ago. The current traditional owners were boys when their fathers executed the last rock paintings on the ceiling of a shelter at Mount Borradaile.

Mount Borradaile is about 40 kilometres north of Gunbalanya, where Aboriginal rock paintings around Paddy Cahill's Oenpelli station were first documented shortly before World War One. The Oenpelli paintings were brought to international fame by Dr. Charles Percy Mountford's grand scientific expedition to Arnhem Land in 1948, covered by The *National Geographic Magazine*. Mountford, though he was not the first to do so, lauded the Oenpelli sites as 'the most numerous and beautiful series of cave paintings that we know of in Australia'. Since then, and particularly in the last thirty years, there has been intense interest in the region's rock art. The substantial inventory of work ensuing from this attention will remain far from comprehensive for a long time to come. The sites around Mount Borradaile remained largely unknown to outsiders until very recently, and there has barely been time for Max Davidson's discoveries to be properly incorporated into that expanding catalogue.

Remarkably then, they have recently become among the more accessible sites of their type. The traditional owners, via Max Davidson, have been inviting non-Aborigines to explore the region by providing guided tours of more than a dozen of the most significant sites in the vicinity of Mount Borradaile. A base-camp, supplied by air and accessible by 4WD, has been built to accommodate visitors, and Max's guides direct small groups to the various locations on a daily basis. The venture, in its short history, has already won several of Australia's most prestigious tourism accolades, including multiple Northern Territory Brolga Awards.

This book, which has been produced with the co-operation and assistance of Max and Philippa Davidson, and with the informed consent of the traditional owners, catalogues and describes some of the main art sites around Mount Borradaile. As an inventory of local rock paintings, it cannot pretend to be exhaustive or complete. Max boasts that one could spend a month with him, rustling through scrub, clambering up steep rocks and navigating dark, narrow passageways, and still only see a fraction of the local paintings. There are some sites which cannot be photographed and some from which non-Aborigines (balanda) are strictly excluded. Moreover, as anyone who accepts the invitation to partake in this unique experience will testify, the photographic record cannot match the effect of surveying the art in its natural environment.

Where possible (or imaginable) we have offered remarks on the meaning and significance of these paintings, though our observations must necessarily remain descriptive and sketchy. More precise understandings of the Mount Borradaile art are no longer possible. The traditions associated with this particular area have mostly passed, while some of the surviving knowledge belongs to the domain of 'secret business'. Moreover, as balanda, our ability to understand such meanings is unavoidably restrained. We have, however, outlined some of the non-Aboriginal methods and theories used to categorise and describe the local rock paintings, and included notes on painting tools and techniques. To help provide some context for the art we offer descriptions of the land and its people, and a short account of the recent contact between the inhabitants and outsiders.

Out of respect for the demands of the traditional Aboriginal owners we have not included a detailed site map, as would normally be expected in a work of this nature, and all care has been taken to avoid reproduction or discussion of confidential paintings and knowledge. The identification of paintings is derived mostly from

Max Davidson catches his breath at the Thylacine Cave. A retired buffalo shooter, Max now runs the multi-award winning Davidson's Arnhem Land Safaris.

Charlie Mangulda and the 'Kakadu Man', Big Bill Neidjie, via Max Davidson. Big Bill's son, Jonathan Nadji* and Peter Rotumah of Jabiru also offered their wisdom and guidance. We are indebted to those who shared their thoughts and expertise, including Josephine Flood, previously of the Australian Heritage Commission, Bob Courtney of the Australian War Memorial, Mark Harvey of Newcastle University, Robert Handelsmann, Ian Hansen of Hunter's Hill, Diane Smith of the Australian National University, Paul S.C. Tacon of the Australian Museum and Margaret 'Peggy' Grove of New College of California. We are also grateful to the Northern Land Council for providing travel permits.

* Note: Big Bill's name is pronounced and commonly spelt Neidjie (as in the *Oxford Companion to Aboriginal Art and Culture*). His son Jonathan, whose Aboriginal name is Yarramarna, spells his name Nadji, an Anglicised spelling of his father's name. Big Bill passed away during the writing of this book. His children, including Jonathon, have allowed authors to use their father's name.

THE LAND
AND ITS PEOPLE

Mount Borradaile rises above the vast plains that stretch between the towering cliffs of the Arnhem Land escarpment and the Arafura Sea. It is one of the more colossal sandstone outliers punctuating the landscape, a battered outcrop left stranded by the retreating escarpment that now lies to the south-east. The plains are dissected by Cooper Creek, which originates in the Spencer Range, spilling from the escarpment through Nimbuwah and Nabarlek. The creek meanders thirty kilometres west of Mount Borradaile, feeding wetlands and paperbark swamps, before converging with the extensive mudflats and mangrove forests of the East Alligator River as it opens into Van Diemen's Gulf.

The region encompasses various ecological zones, mostly low-lying wetlands and savanna woodlands, with pockets of paperbark forest and freshwater lagoons, broken by rocky outliers. Together they sustain an immense variety and density of flora and fauna. The intricate sandstone formations provide an abundance of caves and overhangs that are fit for human use and habitation. The region was, and remains, a most propitious and optimal region for Aboriginal settlement.

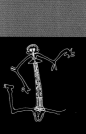

Dawn illuminates the spectacular Cooper Creek wetlands. The brothers Harry and Joe Cooper were Melville Island buffalo shooters from the late 1890s. Joe's son, Reuben Cooper, had a timber camp north of the creek. The paperbark forests that flank the creek accommodate a host of quintessential native species such as the jabiru, whistling kite, white-bellied sea eagle, honeyeaters, rainbow lorikeets, kingfishers and the blue-winged kookaburra. The Prussian explorer, Ludwig Leichhardt, who passed through this region in 1845, observed that the 'cackling of geese, the quacking of ducks, the sonorous note of the native companion, and the noises of black and white cockatoos, and a great variety of other birds, gave the country, both night and day, an extraordinary appearance of animation' (Leichhardt, 1847).

An enormous sandstone boulder, formed from the erosion of the escarpment over countless millennia. The shelter was once used as an occasional living area by Aboriginal people. The native grasses and woodlands surrounding it provided foods, fuels and multiple materials.

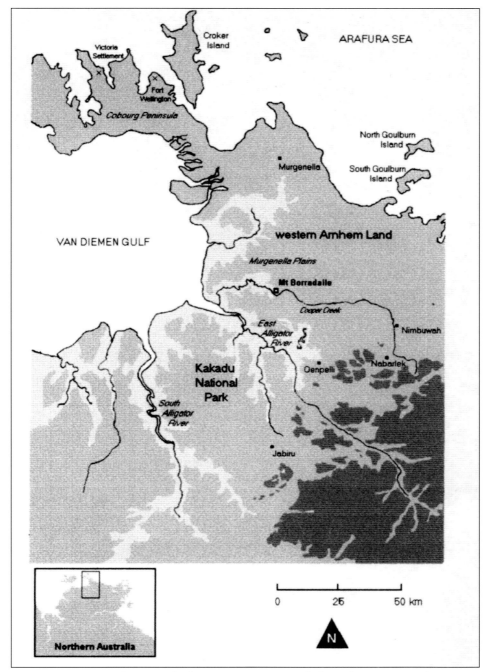

Map 1: Western Arnhem Land, showing Mount Borradaile and Cooper Creek.

The evidence of human habitation is everywhere, but concentrated mostly in the rock-shelters. Some shelters are spacious and secure enough to accommodate reasonably large groups of people. They are refuges during the Wet Season, secure above the floodwaters and affording reliable access to a wide variety of foods, materials and medicines. The floors are scorched from campfires and the ceilings blackened with soot. Mounds of discarded shells (midden heaps) are common, the remains scattered by scrub fowl. The rock floors and platforms are peppered with the smooth holes worn by grinding stones. The walls and ceilings are usually coloured by a layered mosaic of ochre-paintings.

Grinding holes in a habitation shelter at Brolga Camp. The grinding holes are hallmarks of a habitation shelter, indicating the preparation of seeds and grain.

These shelters are the optimum sites for archaeological excavation. Though no scientific tests have been conducted in the immediate vicinity of Mount Borradaile, other sites have thrown light on the activities of many thousands of generations of previous occupants — the food they ate, the tools they forged and the materials they used. The shelters in the Borradaile region reveal surface evidence of material culture in more recent times. Artefacts are strewn about the shelters, or cached in discreet crevices, as in the Artefact Cave, where one bundle of souvenirs and implements resembles a bush toolkit comprising both local and European materials.

Shelter and gallery near the Cooper Creek Lightning Man. The protruding log has been deliberately fastened into a crevice and may have been useful for hanging dilly bags. Its sharpened end suggests it could also have been used for digging.

'The Catacombs' near the Artefact Cave, Mount Borradaile.

Prehistory

The time-span of human occupation in this region incorporated the last phases of the Pleistocene epoch. It has literally been the home of Aboriginal people since time immemorial. Scientific estimates of the antiquity of human occupation in Australia are constantly being revised, though the current weight of evidence, based mostly on excavations at sites in Kakadu National Park, suggests a minimum of 50,000 to 55,000 years.

For much of that time, they inhabited a vastly different environment; one far more distant from the coast, more arid and much colder than the sub-tropical climate of modern times. Key aspects of the contemporary environment and human culture can be traced back to the period of transition between the Pleistocene and Holocene epochs, roughly 15,000 to 6,000 years ago. During this time, temperatures increased and sea levels rose. The receding shorelines closed the land-bridge between northern Australia and New Guinea, and channelled dynamic, tidal rivers across the low-lying plains of western Arnhem Land. A cool, semi-arid woodland habitat was recast into a rich estuarine environment under a monsoonal climate, with the landscape permeated by vast saline flats and dense mangrove swamps.

These climatic and ecological transformations provoked pivotal adjustments to the economy and culture of local Aboriginal society. The migration of displaced coastal peoples and the new resources of an estuarine environment encouraged an increased population. Early in the Estuarine Period, from around 8,000 years ago, there was more intensive and constant occupation of shelters and open sites on the East Alligator River floodplains, evidenced in the increased density of materials and artifacts in the deposits exhumed by archaeologists. This expanding population fostered greater competition for resources and a stricter division of territorial boundaries, reflected in the depictions of conflict and battles in the rock paintings of this period. These ecological changes also promoted the introduction of new technologies. The archaeological deposits reveal important artefactual changes, including the development of stone points for spears. The rock paintings reveal new weapons such as the multi-pronged spear and the spear-thrower.

From around 3,000 to 1,500 years ago, the estuarine environment was modified again by the development of freshwater swamps and billabongs, consequent to the gradual formation of sand levees along the river fronts, which barricaded the tidal incursions on the floodplains, and the flushing and pooling of the Wet Season rains. The freshwater lagoons and billabongs are a key resource for human foragers, with their high concentration of vegetable and animal foods. This heightened abundance resulted in a further, more decisive increase in population, and a corresponding adjustment and diversification of technologies and survival strategies, and new forms of social organisation. This period is believed to have further encouraged the trend toward localised social units and a greater cultural diversity, evidenced in a marked regionalism in the styles and subjects of art produced in the last 1,000 to 2,000 years.

Amurdak

At the time Europeans arrived, western Arnhem Land was a well-settled area, supporting a comparatively high population of accomplished hunters and gatherers who followed refined and well-balanced patterns of living. The broad cultural group of western Arnhem Land Aborigines incorporated several language groups, spoken by a variety of smaller, patrilineal units, or clans, each identified with particular estates and sites. Clans were self-contained, but essentially exogamous, maintaining strong and intricate ties with their neighbours. They united through marriage, trade, shared myths and traditions. They shared resources and combined for ceremonial and secular affairs. There was continuous movement across one another's land, and consequently a number of ways in which identity and relationship to land are defined.

The Mount Borradaile region formed the estates of Amurdak speaking clans. Amurdak was spoken along the eastern shores of Van Diemen Gulf and the East Alligator River, around the lower regions of Cooper and Murgenella Creeks (see Map 2). It was one of the numerous languages detected by the anthropologist Baldwin Spencer at Oenpelli station in 1912, the one he named 'Umoriu' (or Amoordiyu, the Gagadju term for Amurdak), and one of the languages that comprised the vast 'Kakadu Nation', as Spencer termed it (Spencer 1928). The Amurdak-speaking clans were among the numerous local peoples dispersed and decimated by contact, whose language and culture was subsumed early in the twentieth century by the westward expansion of Kunwinjku peoples from the King and Liverpool Rivers. By the time the distinguished anthropologists, Ronald and Catherine Berndt, commenced their studies at Oenpelli in the late 1940s, 'Amurag' or 'Wuraidbuk' (from Wardadjbak, the Kunwinjku term for Amurdak) was among the numerous local languages identified as being severely threatened. There are very few Amurdak speakers today, prompting recent efforts to document the dying language and traditions of the few surviving elders (Handelsman, 1991).

The immediate vicinity of Mount Borradaile belongs to the Bunidj clan, who spoke Amurdak. Bunidj was their gunmogurrgurr, or primary clan name, which they shared with the Gagadju-speaking Bunidj who occupied the opposite side of the East Alligator River, in what is now Kakadu National Park (see Glossary for gunmogurrgurr). There were several other Amurdak-speaking clan groups, identified in the late 1980s by the linguist, Dr. Mark Harvey. There were Amurdak-speaking Gamulgban and Galardju clans whose lands were north of Cooper Creek. The Djindibi clan, who spoke Urrirrk, a dialect of Amurdak, occupied the mouth of Cooper Creek. Sites around the Borradaile airstrip and Davidson's base-camp were the estate of a Malakirri clan, now apparently extinct. Further up the creek, above Mount Borradaile, there were Mirrar and Ulbu clan territories. The most southern Amurdak speakers were Mundarn, who owned much of the East Alligator River above Oenpelli (Harvey, 1992).

Map 2: The languages of western Arnhem Land (from Harvey, 1992; Chaloupka, 1993).
The major languages north of Amurdak, toward the Cobourg Peninsula and the Goulburn Islands, are Iwaidja and Maung. On the western side of the East Alligator, in the current Kakadu National Park, the clans spoke Gagadju and the now extinct Ngaduk language. In the east, around the upper Goomaderr and Liverpool Rivers, they spoke Kunwinjku. South of Amurdak, around Oenpelli and the mid East Alligator River — Magela Creek region, there was Mengerrdji, Erre and Wurningak — dialects of a language known by the Gagadju as Gimbiyu.

A figure in headdress playing didjeridu, Freshwater Period, 75 cm tall. The most famous instrument of Australian Aboriginal society, the drone-pipe or didjeridu, originated in north-western Australia. The aerophone is made most commonly of bamboo, or of eucalypt saplings hollowed by termites, cut between 1-2 metres in length. The rim of the mouthpiece can be moulded with beeswax. The earliest representations of the didjeridu in the rock art of western Arnhem Land belong to the Freshwater Period, positing it as a fairly recent addition to Aboriginal society. The use of the instrument was described with wonder and amusement by early European visitors to the shores of northern Australia. The great range of tonal and rhythmic effects that can be extracted from a hollow tube by a skilful player has endeared the instrument to international fame. In this painting, the player is standing, holding the instrument before him with both hands. The didjeridu is also commonly played sitting down, and sometimes held in one hand, leaving the other free to beat time with a stick.

The 'senior' traditional owner of Mount Borradaile is Charlie Mangulda of the Bunidj clan. Charlie is in his mid-sixties and resides on Croker Island, where he was taken to reside with missionaries around 1947. He was supposed to have been schooled but instead lived 'in the bush' with those Islanders who remained independent of the mission.

Tiger Mungawulu was also removed as a boy. He is an Ulbu clan member whose estates are further up Cooper Creek, above Mount Borradaile. As a young man Tiger worked on a pearling lugger. For around eight years he assisted the famed buffalo shooter and ranger, Frank Woerle, at Cannon Hill and Cobourg. Tiger now lives close-by at Murgenella, north Mount Borradaile.

The Mount Borradaile region also has special significance for the family of the 'Kakadu Man', the late Big Bill Neidjie, of the Gagadju Bunidj clan. Big Bill was born in the 1920s on the East Alligator River at Alawandjawan, where his father, Nardampala, worked for the buffalo shooter, Paddy Cahill, but Bill was raised around Mount Borradaile with his mother's family, who were Amurdak Ulbu. After World War Two, Big Bill travelled and worked in various locations in northern Australia, including a stint as a gardener in Darwin. He returned home in the early 1970s as a main claimant in the Alligator Rivers' Stage II land claim and, until his death in 2002, he was esteemed as a senior elder and custodian of his traditional lands, which now comprise the hub of Australia's most famous National Park. Though he is associated with the Cannon Hill -Ubirr area in Kakadu National Park, Big Bill had an intimate and extensive knowledge of the Borradaile region and was one of the last legatees of the Amurdak language and traditions. His knowledge and his rights are vested in his son, Jonathan.

Another individual associated with the region is Peter Rotumah, a man in his seventies, now living in Jabiru. Peter was born on the coast, his father a shiphand on the mission boat 'Larapang' which ferried supplies from Darwin to Oenpelli. Like Tiger, Peter worked on luggers diving for trochus shell. He is recognised as an Amurdak clansman and an 'owner' of the Amurdak language, though like many of his generation he grew up speaking Iwaidja. 'Iwaidja was spoken by most people then' he recalls. 'Only some old people spoke Amurdak'. Peter has strong familial ties to the Borradaile region (there are handprints in sacred shelters at Mount Borradaile belonging to his brother), and he is the inheritor and trustee of various rights and traditions pertaining to the area.

Mythology and tradition

Western Arnhem Landers are perhaps the most intensively studied Aboriginal peoples in Australia, with a massive corpus of information spanning the entire twentieth century. Yet there are surprisingly few recorded accounts of the traditions associated with the Mount Borradaile region, or at least few from the Amurdak speakers themselves. Most of what we know about traditional society in western Arnhem Land is derived from the study of neighbouring groups, particularly Gagadju, Kunwinjku and Maung. In as much as the Amurdak clans were part of a broader cultural unit, the observations made of their neighbours by anthropologists, missionaries, administrators and travellers, provides some insight into the mythology and tradition of those who lived, danced, sung and painted around Mount Borradaile.

Charlie Mangulda, the senior traditional owner of Mount Borradaile, smoking a crab-claw pipe. Photo by Max Davidson.

The culture and cosmology of western Arnhem Land Aborigines is articulated through a vast and vibrant mythology, sustained by oral tradition and animated through story, song, painting, dance and ritual. The corpus of mythologies that comprise the Dreaming give meaning and purpose to both the physical and spiritual landscapes. They explain and enshrine all patterns of living and behaviour, from codifying domestic and inter-clan socio-economic arrangements to delineating what is edible. Dreaming stories, as they appear to outsiders, are mostly accounts of fantastic, metaphysical characters — powerful Beings and spirits, both benevolent and malignant — who shaped the natural world and imbued it with energy and meaning. Essentially they are travelling stories, of human, animal and metamorphic creatures moving around the country through the territories of various clans and languages, hunting, trading, thieving, fighting, copulating, and usually metamorphosing into some feature on the landscape. Their tracks form a constellation of significant and sacred sites, so that to one skillfully versed in the local mythology, the topography and resources can be read like a map: a 'Speaking Land' (Berndt and Berndt, 1989).

The principal Dreaming character in western Arnhem Land is Warramurrunggundji, the primary progenitor of the land and its people, variously described by anthropologists as the 'First Mother', 'Old Woman', or the 'Fertility' or 'Earth Mother' of western Arnhem Land. Professor Baldwin Spencer's Gagadju informants called her 'Imbromebera' (Spencer, 1928). Among the Kunwinjku she is Yingarna, usually identified as a Rainbow Serpent (Warramurrunggundji was said to be a metamorphosis of Yingarna, or is sometimes said to be Yingarna's daughter). Warramurrunggundji emerged from the northern seas with her partner, Wurragag, her enormous stomach bulging with children. As she travelled through western

Arnhem Land she prepared the land for human habitation, planting vegetable foods and disbursing animals. She then deposited her offspring in strategic sites, allocating them particular languages and totems and instituting their laws and customs. The Mother, in her various guises, is central to the major ritual sequences of western Arnhem Land, in conjunction with other mythical characters such as the Rainbow Serpent, the 'Water Spirit Woman' Ngalkunburriyami, Lumaluma 'the Giant' who instituted the maraiin ceremony, and Yirrbarrdbarrd the 'Snake Man' who is the focus of ubarr fertility rituals (see Glossary).

Most pertinently, the Dreaming is structured knowledge, with layers of detail and meaning ordered by gender, age, social status and personal identity. The Berndts spoke of 'degree of sacredness', but we can more simply delineate between 'public' and 'secret' knowledge. Some of the wisdom pertaining to Mount Borradaile that survives with Charlie Mangulda and the Amurdak clansmen on Croker Island is exceedingly important and extremely secretive. When that knowledge was raised privately amid growing anxiety over proposed mining, forestry and tourism development in the region, subsequent on-site investigations by anthropologists and linguists culminated in the recognition and protection of areas around Mount Borradaile under the Sacred Sites Act. Access to those places is absolutely restricted, as are the surviving traditions associated with them.

Other traditions relating to sites around Cooper Creek are more public, including those reported by the Croker Island minister, Lazarus Lamilami. Though he grew up on the Methodist mission on Goulburn Island, Lamilami was of the mainland, Maung-speaking Manganowal clans, whose lands are north of Cooper Creek. As an old man, Lamilami's outstanding memories of that region were of the caves with 'a lot of bones', and the paintings 'high up in the caves' on unreachable surfaces. One tradition concerned some caves near Mount Borradaile where a large number of people were poisoned by an embittered man named 'Marulda'.

> Not very far from Langa [Mt Permain] is an area we call Igararayi. It is near Mt. Borradaile and in this place there are some caves. There are a lot of bones in the cave, from a lot of people who were killed in there. There was a man called Marulda who got some guiag, a poison, from a place nearby that is djang, and he poisoned all the people who lived in the cave. He knew how to do this thing and how to make the poison and kill these people. He put the poison in the ashes of a fire at the entrance of the cave, and fanned the ashes so all the smoke went into this cave. So all the people died there. He punished them because they wouldn't send him the girl they had promised to him. This poison, it was a very special thing that he knew how to use. But that place where the caves are, that isn't djang. People can go there if they ask Big Nelson, the man who looks after that area (Lamilami, 1974).

The Marulda story is one of a large number of traditions that are shared throughout the region. A Kunwinjku version of the same story was told by the late artist and elder, Nawakadj 'Bobby' Nganjmirra of the Nadjalama clan (Nganjmirra, 1997). Peter Rotumah, an Amurdak elder, is also familiar with this story. His view is that Marulda's woman rejected him because he was sexually inadequate. 'The whole family was

Numerous stone arrangements have been found in western Arnhem Land. These examples near Mount Borradaile are segments of a pathway that extends across many kilometres of Amurdak territory. A similar stone arrangement above Hawk Dreaming, near Cannon Hill, is said to represent piles of fish left by the Dreaming character Garrkanj. In Bulajang country in southern Kakadu, stone pathways leading toward important rock art sites are known to be connected to sacred Bula ceremonies (Gunn, 1992).

against him because of this. That's why he killed them'. He adds that Marulda was executed in retaliation.

Mount Borradaile has strong associations with the mythical character Mabouyou, whose story is highly important to the clans of the western Arnhem Land-Kakadu region. The 'public' version of the story essentially revolves around the theft of Mabouyou's fish by greedy clansmen. Like Marulda, Mabouyou also killed the clan responsible. He located them camped in a cave near Cannon Hill, and sealed the cave entrance with a large rock. This story was current around Oenpelli in the 1950s, when it was related by Gagadju, Mengerdji and Kunwinjku men, who described the main protagonist as a Namorrodo, or dangerous spirit (see Glossary). The story was of particular significance to the 'Kakadu Man', Big Bill Neidjie, whose version is presented at Ubirr rock in Kakadu National Park, and his son Jonathan, who is authorised to 'put his name to it'. Peter Rotumah claims a more authoritative ownership of the story as far as it relates to Mount Borradaile. Peter knows Mabouyou by his Iwaidja name, 'Imbarrbarr'. They have disclosed to the authors that the latter phases of the Mabouyou story pertain to Mount Borradaile, where Mabouyou was killed for his crimes against humans. It is the prerogative of Peter and Jonathan to say as much, but their duty to say no more.

The stories of Marulda and Mabouyou provide a cursory glimpse into a complex and profound cosmology through which Aborigines comprehend and express themselves in relation to their physical and spiritual worlds. Under the aegis of the Dreaming, and in a bountiful environment so skillfully harnessed, they lived a plentiful and secure existence. Ronald and Catherine Berndt, who were not naturally inclined to romanticise Aboriginal society, described the condition of the western Arnhem Landers succinctly:

'... their life was full, and they obtained virtually all they desired. They grew, loved and died believing themselves to be part of a comprehensible and universal scheme arranged primarily for their benefit. There was no real strangeness, no grappling with essentially unknown elements, nor unforseen conditions. They were sure of themselves, and of the culture in which they had grown; they could cope with all they met, all they saw and all they heard. There was no real struggle for survival ... of the kind that we ourselves know in our own mechanised and highly complex culture; no extreme poverty, nor monopolisation.'

The 'delicate balance' of Aboriginal society was 'sharply upset' by the coming of Balanda (Berndt and Berndt, 1974).

A boulder peppered with small cupule engravings. These are approximately 1.0-1.5 cms in width and depth. In the upper centre of the picture is a series of larger, circular petroglyphs (designs pecked, scratched, abraded or cut into the rock surface). Here a pair of parallel, circular lines have been carved, containing some 25 individual cupules. The design bears similarities to others composed of beeswax pellets which are common in the region (see Chapter 3). Petroglyphs are not common in the Borradaile area, though dozens of examples have been found nearby in Kakadu National Park.

Horse shoe, quartz-grinding stones and a buffalo horn.
Aborigines were critical to the local buffalo trade. The labour intensive industry could not have been sustained without them. Large parties were required to skin, wash and cure the hides, while entire communities were drawn to the buffalo camps for trade and employment. Reuben Cooper, son of a Melville Island buffalo shooter, had a timber camp near Mount Borradaile. Charlie's father worked for him as a young man. Reuben, whose mother was Aboriginal, was remembered as being 'very kind to the Aboriginal people', driving them to ceremony and hunts in his old truck (Lamilami, 1974).

knew the pipe, tobacco, bread, rice, ponies, [and] guns'. Leichhardt, who frequently boasted an extensive acquaintance with the customs and manners of Australian Aborigines, thought them 'the most confiding, intelligent, inquisitive natives I had ever met' (Leichhardt, 1847).

New waves of northern exploration and settlement ensued after 1863, when the administration of the Northern Territory became the responsibility of the government of South Australia. Among these was one, in 1874, that ended in tragedy. An Englishman, Edward Sydney Borradaile, had been persuaded to join an Irish entrepreneur, trader and adventurer named Permain, on a prospecting search for minerals, buffalos and pastoral land. Borradaile was a 29 year old civil engineer and draughtsman, appointed to the Lands Office in the Northern Territory. He and Permain departed with two months supplies packed on Timor Ponies, intending to walk overland to the Cobourg Peninsula. They were last seen at Pine Creek, where an old prospector, Charles Gore, tried unsuccessfully to dissuade them from proceeding, on account of the hostile reputation of Aborigines in that country. What became of the two men was not firmly established at the time. Search parties failed to find any trace of them, but it was concluded that they had been robbed and killed by Aborigines of the East Alligator River, somewhere near Tor Rock. Two hills in the vicinity of Tor Rock were named Mount Borradaile and Mount Permain by the South Australian government in commemoration of the missing explorers. Some years later, the prospector Charles Gore was shown a site on the upper East Alligator (south of Mount Borradaile), where he found the remains of the explorers' campsite. Later, while on a trading trip up the East Alligator, Gore bought a silver watch chain that he recognised as Sydney Borradaile's. The story of the murders was recalled by older Aboriginal men in the region at the turn of the century (Spillett, 1982).

From the 1880s there was increasing European activity in western Arnhem Land, with trepangers and beachcombers scouring the coasts and rivers, and buffalo shooters roaming the plains. It was the water buffalo that eventually drew balanda to Amurdak territory. Buffalo were first released by the British garrisons on the Peninsula in the 1820s and 1840s. By the time the northern settlements were abandoned, they had spread south across the Murgenella Plains, where Leichhardt's party hunted one (just north of Mount Borradaile) in 1845, 'a most fortunate event' for the hungry explorers. The Aboriginal men (probably Amurdak-speakers) who joined the feed called the buffalo 'Anaborro', or 'Devil devil' (Leichhardt, 1847). Buffalo shooters were working around the East and South Alligator Rivers and the Cobourg Peninsula from the 1870s, a trade bolstered by the market for meat on the gold fields at Pine Creek. The most famous shooter, Paddy Cahill, hunted both sides of the East Alligator River from the 1890s, initially working from a station at Alawarndjawarn in Amurdak territory. In the hey-day of the buffalo trade, Cahill was the man who epitomised it, becoming widely and famously known as a gallant frontier bushman.

The buffalo era marked the beginnings of a decisive and calamitous upheaval in local Aboriginal society that decimated some local groups like the Gagadju and Amurdak-speaking clans. The escalating presence of Europeans provided a mixture of opportunity and dependence, as Aborigines, motivated by a variety of economic and social incentives, actively sought (and to some degree were forced) to incorporate European ways and resources. Amurdak peoples had been among the large numbers of Aborigines migrating west into Palmerston (Darwin) and the nascent mining towns between the Adelaide River and Pine Creek from the 1870s. Now they were drawn to the buffalo camps for trade and employment. In the ensuing decades, the profusion of new stations and settlements provoked critical demographic shifts, as Aborigines moved out of their traditional estates and other clans were drawn into the region. This coincided with (and contributed to) a dramatic decline in population caused chiefly through exposure to epidemics of influenza, tuberculosis, measles and venereal disease, aggravated by smallpox epidemics (introduced by the Macassans) and leprosy, which came into northern Australia from Asia from the 1870s.

Man smoking a pipe, Major Art shelter.
Tobacco was introduced by the Macassan traders, but it is more associated with the buffalo era, when it was the staple wage paid to Aboriginal shooters and labourers. This figure is probably balanda (non-Aboriginal) because he is wearing shoes. He has his hand on his hip in a pose suggestive of the powerful boss. Above him to the right are two more representations of a pipe.

This painting has been identified as a representation of
Darwin wharf (Chaloupka, 1993). On the lower right side
is a small beeswax design.

When Paddy Cahill settled more permanently at Oenpelli to administer an
experimental farm on behalf of the Northern Territory administration from around
1916, his station, the primary European outpost between Mary River and the Cobourg
Peninsula, became a focal point of local Aboriginal society, where they obtained food,
tobacco, medicine, tools and employment. In 1925, Oenpelli station was handed over
to the Anglican Church Missionary Society, who were less generous in their material
offerings to local Aborigines and took a more interventionist stance against traditional
Aboriginal culture. There was, in the short term, a renewed exodus to other stations
on the 'buffalo plains' to the west (along the Mary and Wildman Rivers), followed by
a drift into the mission, as Aborigines sought to 'fill the gap' left by the decline of the
buffalo industry and the abolition of the Macassan trade (Berndt and Berndt, 1954).
During World War II, the stationing of large numbers of RAAF and Navy personnel at
bases such as those near Oenpelli and on Goulburn Island, further shattered the
relative isolation of western Arnhem Landers, raising new opportunities for trade and
employment but intensifying the physical and cultural damage of foreign intrusion.
The war years also furthered the process of dispersal through the systematic removal
of Aborigines from the northern coastal regions into camps at Adelaide River,
Katherine and Cullen River.

The Contact Period in western Arnhem Land was enormously disruptive and damaging, though generally less so than in most other corners of the continent. The pre-eminent theme of the era is not the destruction of local Aboriginal society and culture, but its survival, acknowledged and sustained by the formal designation of the region as Aboriginal Reserve (from 1931) and, more critically, by the recognition of continuing economic and spiritual ties and traditional ownership under the 1976 Land Rights Act. Today, balanda infiltrate the region in greater numbers than ever before, though they enter strictly under the terms and conditions imposed by the traditional owners. Visitors to Mount Borradaile come not as plunderers exploiting the local resources at the expense of its Aboriginal owners, but as privileged guests, embracing an Aboriginal invitation to experience and enjoy.

Two pistols, near the Thylacine Cave.

The 'tool kit', Artefact Cave, near Mount Borradaile.
This cache of possessions, stashed in a rock crevice near the Major Art habitation site, comprises indigenous and introduced materials/objects. The former includes a ball of beeswax about the size of a cricket ball, a piece of graphite, some haematite, an object that looks like a loom shuttle (probably of ceremonial significance) and a small scraping tool made of wallaby teeth set in beeswax. 'Contact items' include a Macassan adze, a domino, a tobacco pipe of hollowed timber, a bag of shot (partially rotted), and some hand-forged nails and screws. The small tin box contains granules of the bleaching agent, Reckitt's Blue. Dr. Alan White, a Chartered Patent Attorney of Surrey (UK) has identified the embossed trade mark as belonging to the match manufactures Bell and Black of London in the 1870s. A stirrup-buckle, spear-head and a screw-top bottle lid were found on the ground nearby.

THE ROCK PAINTINGS OF WESTERN ARNHEM LAND

The slanting roofs and sides were one mass of native drawings, precisely similar to those done on bark, but, here, the rocks had been blackened for long years by the smoke of countless camp fires and the drawings, most of them fishes, had been superimposed on one another, the brighter colours of the more recent ones standing out clearly on the dark background. Here and there were groups of stencilled hands and feet.

Baldwin Spencer, describing a rock-shelter
near Oenpelli station (Spencer, 1928).

For most of the millennia of human settlement in this region, the inhabitants recorded their presence through the medium of ochre and stone. Excavations in shelters in Kakadu National Park have uncovered samples of ochre, and stones used for grinding ochre, in deposits dated at over 50,000 years old. Ochre was used for other purposes, like body and implement painting, and though the point remains speculative and the subject of dispute, the practice of painting on rock-walls almost certainly dates from this time.

Closer analysis of the relative frequency of ochre pigments in different levels of deposits suggests that rock painting may not have been undertaken consistently

throughout the millennia, but instead occurred in 'bursts' or periods of high production (Tacon and Brockwell, 1995). In some measure, this helps account for the variety of distinct styles in the region's rock paintings. In any event, the western Arnhem Landers, still painting with ochre and handmade brushes, can be regarded as the practitioners of the world's longest continuing painting tradition.

Interpreting western Arnhem Land rock paintings: the 'rock art sequence'

The earliest attempts to classify and interpret the rock paintings of western Arnhem Land were made during the American-Australian Scientific Expedition to Oenpelli in 1948, when Charles Mountford, the expedition leader, and Frederick David McCarthy, the Curator of Anthropology at the Australian Museum, studied the galleries around the Oenpelli mission. Mountford broadly distinguished between the reddish, haematite figures and outlines, and the multi-coloured or polychromatic art which often featured the representation of the subject's internal organs and skeletal structure. The older monochromic art, Mountford was told, was the work of 'a fairy-like invisible people called the mimi' (Mountford, 1956). His notion that these paintings were the work of 'an extinct cultural group' predating modern Aboriginal peoples, was firmly and substantively repudiated by succeeding anthropologists (Mountford, 1956; Berndt, 1958).

Since the mid 1960s, the rock art of the Kakadu — western Arnhem Land region has attracted more detailed attention from scholars such as Eric Brandl and Robert Edwards. The pre-eminent scholar in the field is George Chaloupka formerly of the Museum and Art Gallery of the Northern Territory, who has been documenting rock art sites for over forty years. His thesis, most thoroughly explored in *Journey in Time* (1993), examines Arnhem Land rock paintings within a framework meshed of climatological, palaeoecological, archaeological and historical data. It has been the foundation of more recent work by Josephine Flood, Ivan Haskovec, David Welch, Paul Tacon, Chris Chippindale and Darrell Lewis (see Selected Sources and Further Reading).

Though no such tests have been conducted around Mount Borradaile, rock paintings can sometimes be directly dated through radiocarbon analysis of organic materials captured in pigments, or of the silica and oxalate crusts on painted rock surfaces. The processes of direct dating, however, are fraught with technical and interpretive difficulties, and are only beginning to contribute to the dating of rock paintings in western Arnhem Land. In particular, radiocarbon testing of some 600 examples of beeswax art in Kakadu National Park and central Arnhem Land has provided invaluable evidence of the antiquity and chronology of various images and styles (Nelson et al., 1995).

Instead, the dating, classification and interpretation of rock paintings is generally based on the more human procedures of close and careful observation. Analysis centres on discerning and classifying distinct painting forms and styles, and on examining the superimposition of works within a rock art panel to establish the order in which paintings were executed. Sometimes, distinctive styles and subjects can be correlated with environmental and archaeological data to produce general (sometimes more definite) calculations of antiquity. For instance, paintings depicting the thylacine are reasonably assumed to be older than 4,000 years, when the species

	TABLE 1	
	THE 'ROCK ART SEQUENCE'	
		STYLES/MOTIFS
up to 55,000 years	PRE-ESTUARINE PERIOD	earliest thrown object prints, grass strikings and hand prints
15,000	end of last glaciation temperatures warming; sea levels rising	Large Naturalistic figures
10,000		Dynamic Figures
8,000	ESTUARINE PERIOD	Post Dynamic and Simple Figures with boomerangs and spears; Yam Figures; boomerang stencils; naturalistic estuarine figures; earliest Rainbow Serpent and X-ray paintings
6,000	sea level reaches current level	spear-throwers and composite spears
3,000	RECENT — FRESHWATER PERIOD	Complete Figure Style: Full Figure paintings of fauna, humans and mythical beings, with 'descriptive X-ray' and solid/stroke in-fill designs; beeswax compositions; goosewing fans; magpie geese; didjeridus
300		Contact Phase: foreign objects/animals; sorcery figures

The rock art sequence can be broadly divided into at least three phases: old, intermediate and recent. These correspond with the three major geomorphological periods: the Pre-Estuarine, Estuarine and Freshwater Periods. The oldest art was doubtlessly produced during the Pre-Estuarine era, more than 10,000 years ago. An intermediate phase of rock painting ensued from the end of the last glacial age, from around 10,000 to 6,000 years ago, corresponding with and reflecting the profound environmental and cultural changes wrought by the transition from the Pleistocene to the Holocene era. The more recent phase of rock painting developed in the last 3,000 years, and includes the styles and motifs of the Freshwater Period.

was thought to have been made extinct in mainland Australia by the arrival of the dingo. Other subjects, like the magpie goose, pertain to the Freshwater Period of the last few millennia. There is also the distinctive art of the Contact Period, depicting ships, water buffalo and Martini-Henry rifles, which can be more or less anchored to certain decades of the last 150 years.

The scientific record, combined with the invaluable cultural knowledge afforded by traditionally-orientated Aboriginal informants, provides 'an unusually strong framework' for interpreting and dating the rock art of western Arnhem Land (Chippindale and Tacon, 1998). Though there is some divergence of opinion and a likelihood that fresh evidence will occasion further refinements and revisions in the near future, the overview presented above may be accepted as a synthesis of the various interpretations.

Hand prints and stencils

The earliest rock paintings were the most basic and unsophisticated forms, including thrown-object prints, commonly found high on walls and ceilings, as well as grass prints or 'strikings', and hand prints. Hand stencils probably emerged later in the Pre-Estuarine Period. Hand prints and stencils are, from appearance alone, almost impossible to date, though some are obviously very old. There is no certainty that any of the surviving examples in this area were among the earliest rock paintings, rendered up to 55,000 years ago. That possibility, however, cannot be entirely ruled out. There is at least one local example of the distinctive 'three middle fingers' (3MF) design, associated with early human figures, thought to be over 10,000 years old. Prints and stencils, especially of hands, occur throughout the rock art sequence. Indeed, Charlie Mangulda's hand print was the last known painting executed in this region.

Whereas rock painting was generally the province of men, hand prints and stencils were sometimes rendered by women and children. They were signatures; the brand of a particular individual who may have had special associations with the particular area, or who was a significant visitor, executing a hand stencil to record their presence at a particular site. Many recently painted stencils in the Mount Borradaile region are beautifully and elaborately enhanced by intricate, multi-coloured in-fill patterns, occasionally accentuated with daubs of beeswax. The 'decorative' hand stencils were an innovation confined to western Arnhem Land, and a particular specialty of the Amurdak artists. In some cases, such embellishments, mostly

Grass prints, hand prints and white female figures at Brolga Camp.
The female figures are recent paintings, similar to ones found around Ubirr in Kakadu National Park. They contrast with the hand and grass prints that are characteristic of the oldest art forms of the Pre-Estuarine Period. While the hand prints are evidently old, the grass prints (or 'strikings') are surprisingly recent, appearing over the white pigment of the females. They are the most recent addition to this panel and perhaps among the last paintings executed around Brolga Camp, intimating a recent, perhaps singular revival of the most ancient form of rock art (Tacon, pers.com).

clan/moiety designs, were added to a plain stencil after the person who executed that stencil had died (Forge, 1991). Other examples are thought to mimic laced gloves worn by European women (Chaloupka, 1993).

Hand stencils dominate a shelter adjoining the Mount Borradaile Rainbow Serpent site. On the top right is the stencil of a child. The stencil next to it exemplifies the three middle fingers (3MF) design, in which the artist pressed his middle fingers together to create the resemblance of an emu's foot. The design, which is found throughout the Arnhem Land region, is associated with the Dynamic Figures phase of the Pre-Estuarine Period, and believed to be over 10,000 years old.

A line of hand stencils on the ceiling of a shelter, several metres above the ground. Each stencil is apparently made by the same artist, judging by the clenched or missing forefinger.

Charlie Mangulda's hand print.

Decorated hand stencils, one with Reckitt's Blue, overlying layers of figurative art in the
Major Art habitation shelter. A number of the hand stencils have borders around them in
what is possibly an attempt to distinguish them from their immediate environment.
Unusually, the hand stencil on the bottom left has two borders around it.

Decorated hand-stencil, enclosed in a 'frame'.

Decorated hand stencil, next to what might be an attempt to write the numerals '82', Contact Wall, Mount Borradaile.

Styles of the Pre-Estuarine Period

The primal, elemental art of hand and object prints was succeeded by large, naturalistic representations of animals. The earliest paintings were mostly of macropods, depicting the predominant species of a semi-arid, inland environment. The sweeping term, 'Large Naturalistic Figures complex' (Chaloupka, 1993)

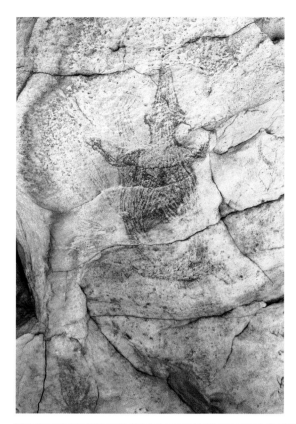

A naturalistic painting of a freshwater or Johnston crocodile (Crocodylus johnstonii), near the Mount Borradaile Rainbow Serpent shelter. The freshwater crocodile is distinguished by its narrow snout, and grows to about three metres in length.

A short-eared rock wallaby in the naturalistic style, from a gallery near the Paperbark Beds habitation site.

categorises various distinct stylistic forms, some of which are evidently more recent. Paintings in this style consist of broad, fluent outlines, sometimes in-filled with contour lines or ochre wash. They demonstrate particular attention to those details which are defining characteristics of a species, like the plumage of an emu, the long neck of a turtle or the caudal and dorsal fins of a barramundi. The depiction of now-extinct faunal species like thylacine and Tasmanian Devil bolsters the estimation that some of the naturalistic fauna painting is considerably old.

The illustration of human figures emerged in the latter stages of the Pre-Estuarine Period. The earliest are regarded as among 'the most vital and exciting' works of local rock art — the 'Dynamic Figures' (Chaloupka, 1993). These are monochrome, fine-brush drawings, mostly human and mostly male, with some animals and therianthropes (composite human/animal figures). They are distinguished by their animated poses, a 'feeling for composition and movement' (Mountford, 1956), depicting hunting, conflict and ceremonial scenes. These paintings frequently illustrate weapons and material objects, including various types of spears, boomerangs, stone axes, digging sticks and dilly bags, as well as human apparel such as headdresses, tassels, armlets, pendants and pubic aprons. The antiquity of the Dynamic Figures style is evident in the extent of its spatial distribution. The figures are found throughout western and central Arnhem Land, and as far west as the Cadell River, exhibiting a remarkable uniformity of design and theme. They are reflective of a more widely spread, more itinerant and more homogeneous people.

Dynamic Figure, Artefact Cave. This beautifully drawn haematite figure in headdress is a consummate example of the Dynamic Figure style. He carries a boomerang and is probably hunting. The right arm is raised, as if throwing a weapon, though the weapon is obscured by another painting.

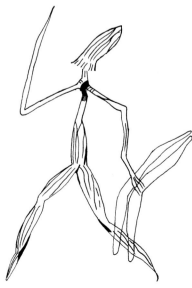

In the more remote caves we found a different form of art. This, the native men explained, was not the work of their ancestors, but of a tall, thin bodied, mythical race called the Mimi. No Aborigine has seen a Mimi; these mysterious people with particularly keen hearing escape into the hills when strangers approach. They live among rock clefts, venturing abroad only on calm days, lest the wind break their fragile bones.

Charles Percy Mountford

Styles of the Intermediate or early Estuarine Phase

The art of the early Estuarine Period, from around 8,000 years ago, reflects the changing regional environment and the consequent adaptation and modification of human society. The peoples of western Arnhem Land now inhabited a landscape fashioned by higher rainfalls, tidal rivers, saline swamps and extensive mangrove forests. Human settlement patterns intensified, new technologies and strategies were adopted and there was increasing diversity and regionalisation within the broader cultural group.

In the art of the early Estuarine Period, the transition was marked, in some measure, by continuity, as in the persisting tradition of naturalistic animal paintings. They were now frequently smaller, and depicted new estuarine species such as barramundi, mullet, saltwater crocodile and catfish. Some of the peculiar, large naturalistic human figures date at least from this period, though they may be considerably older. The period was marked by a simplification of painted human figures. In the 'Post-Dynamic Figure', 'Simple Figure' (Chaloupka, 1993) and 'Northern Running Figure' (Haskovec, 1992) styles, human forms progressively became less dynamic and more stylised, developing into front-on stick-figures and silhouettes painted in thick, single brushstrokes. These

A beautifully executed short-eared rock wallaby (Petrogale brachyotis), painted near the Cooper Creek swimming hole. Note the detail in the fore and hind legs.

Large human figures.
Paintings of this nature are rare. These human figures are remarkably large, bearing some marks of the old Large Naturalistic style of fauna painting. Other examples of large human outlines have been found as far away as the Arnhem Land plateau above Jim Jim Creek, and are probably associated with the Yam period, between 4,000 to 6,000 years of age (Tacon, pers.com).

comparatively rudimentary figures, however, retained their rich and detailed depiction of material culture. They record the endurance of older traditions, as in the manufacture and use of headdresses and tassels. Later in the Estuarine Period, from around 6,000 years ago, the evolving landscape and human technologies were depicted in the decline of subjects like the thylacine and boomerang, and the first appearance of the fighting pick and spear-thrower

The transformation and adjustment of Aboriginal society during the early Estuarine Period also generated 'the most enigmatic images in rock art anywhere in the world', in the so-called the 'Yam Figures' style (Chaloupka, 1993). This began with elementary depictions of yams, evolving into complex representations of yam-like human and animal figures — a decisive shift in style from naturalism to symbolism that was indicative of maturing metaphysical consciousness. The earliest Rainbow Serpents and some of the first X-ray paintings are associated with this period. Recent studies have determined that the Yam Figures were, at least for a time, produced concurrently with Post-Dynamic and Simple Figures, which were formerly believed to be an older style. The Simple Figures therefore probably illustrate practical and secular activities/concerns such as hunting and fighting, while the Yam Figures 'depict activities in a spiritual domain' (Chippindale and Tacon, 1998).

The Recent / Freshwater Period

The Recent Period, from around 3,000 years ago, produced the most prolific phase of rock painting, and spawned the most diverse and elaborate forms of local rock art. The Freshwater Period, in geomorphological terms, covers the last 1,500 years, and the subject matter of paintings reflect the emergence of a new ecosystem featuring species such as the long-necked turtle (Chelodina rugosa), magpie goose (Anseranus semipalmatta) and whistling duck (Dendrocygna sp.). For the first time, human figures are depicted with didjeridus and clap-sticks, indicating significant changes in the local traditions of music and song. The Recent Period saw the maturation of X-ray paintings and the emergence of internal or in-fill patterning, including rarrk (cross-hatching), praised by Frederick McCarthy as 'one of the most interesting technical developments in Australian cave art' (McCarthy, 1962), and perpetuated in the bark and paper paintings of contemporary Arnhem Land artists.

An overwhelming proportion of the surviving rock paintings around Mount Borradaile belong to the Recent/Freshwater Period. The range of subjects and designs are more 'open-ended' than in the earlier conventions, and there is more superimpositioning of paintings, so that the older styles tend to be isolated and preserved, while the recent ones jostle for space in clusters. Corresponding with the increasing diversity and regionalism of Aboriginal society in the western Arnhem Land/Kakadu region, this period saw the emergence of distinct, localised painting traditions, with definable differences in motif, style and pigment selection in various localities (Tacon, 1992).

On a regional level, several distinct art-forms were produced contemporaneously. Paul Tacon, who has studied the Recent Period paintings closely, classifies them collectively under the banner 'Complete Figure Style' (Tacon, 1992). They included smaller, monochromatic 'stick-figure' paintings of (mostly) male figures, often in energetic postures, sometimes composed in hunting, ceremonial and fighting scenes. (The renowned stick figure paintings around Gunbalanya portray hunters and dancers with goosewing fans and didjeridus). The trademark paintings of the Recent Period are the 'Full Figures': monochomatic and polychromic paintings depicting all manner of fauna, humans and mythical beings, with X-ray features and solid/stroke in-fill patterns. The Full Figure human paintings of the Recent Period are distinctive and widespread. They have long, supple bodies with contorted limbs, 'floating' on the rock walls in postures suggestive of dancing and sex. Most human figures have female characteristics — elongated breasts and enlarged vulva. Male figures are also unambiguously indicated by exaggerated genital details. There was also a continuing tradition of hand/object stencils and prints, sometimes with X-ray features like finger-bones, as well as elaborate and colourful prints, in-filled with strokes and dots. Innovations of the period included beeswax compositions.

X-ray and decorative in-fill paintings

X-ray painting is so named because of its depiction of internal features. The most commonly represented features are the backbone and digestive tract, though there are occasional illustrations of the heart, lungs/air sac, liver, kidney, diaphragm, body fat, muscles and optic nerves. X-ray paintings are found in many other examples of ancient art in northern Europe, Spain, Siberia, North America, New Guinea and Malaysia. In western Arnhem Land, early and relatively simplistic examples are exhibited in monochromatic paintings dating from the early Estuarine Period, around 8,000 years ago, though these are rare. The X-ray convention was far more prominent in the later phases of the rock art sequence, developing and culminating in the works of the Freshwater Period.

The recent X-ray style of painting incorporates the distinctive 'decorative' work in which spaces within the figure are in-filled with solid bodies of colour, dots and/or

A monochrome painting of a barramundi near the Cooper Creek Lightning Man. Note the contrasting use of solid and stroke in-fill.

elaborate parallel hatching and cross-hatching (rarrk). The term 'decorative', in the sense of being purely ornamental, is a misnomer. The fine, detailed patterns are clan and moiety designs: complex personal and group signatures related to body designs worn during sacred rituals, possibly derived from the patterns on plant leaves (Chaloupka, 1993). Moreover, in local art the visual brilliance of colour and intricate patterning communicates Aboriginal perceptions of life-essence. As Paul Tacon explains, it reflects an abstract, metaphoric association of life with colour and radiance, epitomised by the complexion of fish scales and snake skins, glistening when the creature is alive, turning sallow and opaque when it dies. In the natural, physical environment, colour reaches its zenith in the appearance of a rainbow — a potent and pervasive symbol in Aboriginal cosmology. Colour, or 'rainbow-ness', signifies the potency of life and the vitality of nature (Tacon, 1992).

The X-ray and in-fill techniques are perpetuated by modern Kunwinjku artists, and observations of their work by Luke Taylor, Paul Tacon, Peter Carroll and others have provided some conceptions relating to Recent Period rock paintings. In modern Kunwinjku art , for instance, X-ray figures are associated with the secular concerns of hunting and food preparation, whereas figures in-filled with rarrk take on 'ancestral overtones'. A painting of a kangaroo with X-ray features may be 'just a tucker kangaroo', whereas one with rarrk patterning is a 'Dreaming kangaroo' with special and sacred meanings (Taylor, 1982). Some rock paintings of animals that are composed of solid or stroke in-fill designs, without internal features, are identified by contemporary Aboriginal informants as portrayals of dead or cooked animals, as opposed to those with X-ray features, which are said to be living creatures (Tacon, 1988).

Most X-ray paintings depict local fauna and aquatic species. The depictions of humans do not normally portray internal organs (heart, lungs, kidney, etc), though the Mount Borradaile paintings frequently depict backbones and what we take to be optic nerves. Paintings of humans tend to focus more on external features such as tassels. One contemporary Aboriginal explanation for this omission is that it deprives malevolent spirits of the opportunity to draw sustenance from human organs (Tacon, 1988).

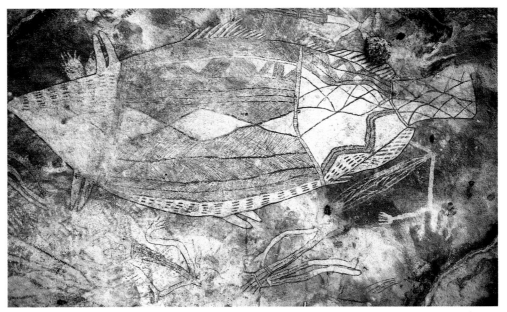

A Recent Period painting of a barramundi (Lates calcarifer), on the underbelly of Jabiru Rock, lower Cooper Creek. This is an eminent example of the use of 'decorative' in-fill, laden with sacred meanings. Barramundi are a popular food for local Aborigines. They also feature prominently in the traditional belief systems of this area. In an old Mengerrdji (Oenpelli) tradition, a Dreaming Barramundi was speared by Aboriginal hunters, but escaped and retreated toward the coast, making the East Alligator River as he fled. He metamorphosed into a rock at the mouth of the river at Gulari Point, where he can still be seen at low tide. Several versions of this story were told in the 1940s-50s, including one by Kunwinjku women at Oenpelli, who knew the Dreaming Barramundi as 'Namangal' (Berndt and Berndt, 1989).

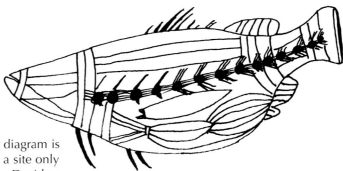

An X-ray barramundi. This diagram is of a painting at 'New Art', a site only recently discovered by Max Davidson some distance south of Mount Borradaile. This appears a very recent work, painted on a bold white background. Lacking the intricate and complex patterning of some Recent Period paintings, this one may be a 'tucker' barramundi. Note how the defining characteristics of the species are clearly indicated, including the distinctly pointed head and extended jaw, and the several spiky spines of the front dorsal fin.

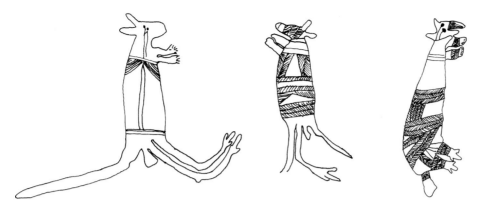

Recent Period wallaby paintings from the Mount Borradaile region, illustrating the use of solid and stroke in-fill. They are in strong contrast to the naturalistic fauna paintings of an earlier era.

Recent Period anthropomorphic figure, red ochre outline and detail on a white silhouette, her gender conspicuously indicated. The human figures in this style hover on the walls in bizarre, impossible postures.

Painting of an inverted rifle, Major Art site. This painting lies obscured at
the bottom of the main wall of the shelter.

The Art of the Contact Period

Association with outsiders and the consequent introduction of objects, subjects
and knowledge, is reflected in a profusion of 'Historical Paintings', or 'Contact Art'.
The art of the Contact Period can be divided into two overlapping categories —
Macassan and European. Examples of both abound throughout the region, though
around Mount Borradaile the paintings mostly reflect the European influence. Locally,
there are two particular sites — a wall at Mount Borradaile, and the Major Art shelter
— that feature a concentration of contact art. The range of subjects is considerable,
though by far the most prolific are the ship and rifle.

The prominence of ships and firearms in the contact paintings of Kakadu and
western Arnhem Land attests to their importance as defining symbols of the
technology and culture of balanda. An early introduction to both subjects occurred
simultaneously in 1818 when the British navigator, Lt. Philip King, explored the
northern shores in the 84 ton cutter, the Mermaid. King's men, while paddling up a
narrow inlet at Knocker's Bay, were showered with spears thrown by unseen
assailants. The English responded with a 'volley of musketry into the mangroves'.

Few guns or ships were seen south of the Cobourg Peninsula during the colonial
era, though Amurdak clansmen undoubtedly observed both in great detail during
visits to the early British settlements. Most of the Borradaile contact paintings belong
to the decades surrounding the turn of the twentieth century, when European
trepangers and pearlers plied the coastlines and buffalo shooters roamed the
mainland plains. The ship paintings are mostly of the type of sloops, cutters and
ketches that were frequently seen on the East Alligator River during the buffalo era,
when they serviced the ventures of men like Fred Smith at Kapalga, Reuben Cooper,
Paddy Cahill and (from 1925) the missionaries at Oenpelli.

The firearm paintings are predominantly of Martini-Henry rifles, widely used by mounted troops and police in the Australian colonies from around 1875, and the badge of the local buffalo industry around the turn of the twentieth century. There are a number of pistol paintings, some of which may be percussion action, single shot muzzle loaders of the type used by military and colonial police authorities during the 1840s. At a time when the East Alligator River clans were considered 'wild' and hostile, Aboriginal access to firearms was cautiously restricted, though Aborigines who worked in the industry were famed for their bravery and talent as shooters. Some rifle paintings around Mount Borradaile indicate a sound familiarity with, and probable ownership of, such weapons. One old, rusted Martini-Henry has been found stashed in a local shelter.

While the Aboriginal experience of European weaponry was mostly a product of their employment in the buffalo industry, the role of firearms as a weapon of conquest cannot be ignored. By the time Europeans came to exploit the resources of western Arnhem Land, the manner of engaging local Aboriginal populations had been hardened by a century of intolerance and persecution. A long frontier tradition of indiscriminate murder by punitive parties persisted in some remoter regions of Australia well into the twentieth century. On all the Cobourg Peninsula settlements during the 1820s-40s, relations between the British and local Aborigines deteriorated,

Rifles and pistols surrounded by hand stencils, Major Art shelter. Here are two beautifully painted Martini-Henry rifles, and two percussion-cap pistols. Great attention to detail has been shown. Important mechanical parts such as the triggers and adjustable sights have been accurately painted, certifying the artist's familiarity with these particular firearms. Curiously the rifles have been painted upside down, as they might look when carried by an untrained user, or when hung on a wall, dangling by the straps like a basket or dilly bag. The percussion-cap pistols are distinguishable by the small protruding mount on which the cap was placed. The powder ignited when the hammer struck the cap. The percussion-cap superceded the flint-lock. It was more accurate, less susceptible to moisture and the caps could be conveniently bought in tins. They were popular until the1860s, though in remote areas their use may have persisted much longer. Possibly, the pistol paintings around Mount Borradaile are a reflection of contact with military personnel pre. 1870, when revolvers became standard military issue.

at some point, into exchanges of bullets and spears, with at least one brutal massacre by soldiers and armed convicts from Fort Wellington, on a beach at Bowen Strait in 1827 (Sweatman, in Allen and Corris, 1977). Later, numerous attacks on overland exploring parties, and the disappearance of Permain and Borradaile, won the Aborigines of the East Alligator River region the reputation of being fierce and militant. The reported murder of Permain and Borradaile aroused a casual and typical demand for vengeance,'to teach these Alligator blacks that they cannot perpetuate such crimes unpunished' (*Northern Territory Times*, 20 March 1875). Later that year, an explorer/pastoralist, John Lewis, was engaged in series of affrays with Aborigines near the East Alligator, that wear the unmistakable air of slaughter (Lewis, 1922). The ensuing host of traders, hunters and speculators who pursued their endeavours in western Arnhem Land around the turn of the twentieth century were mostly remembered as cruel and brutal characters, and some, like Ronnie Spenser and Jimmy Campbell, were killed by Aborigines. Another, Joe Cooper, who was based on Melville Island, was said to have poisoned two men with laced damper and jam in random retaliation for the theft of stores (Lamilami, 1974).

One of the more conspicuous indications of foreign contact in local Aboriginal rock painting is the use of the laundry product, Reckitt's Blue or 'washing blue', manufactured in the United States until early in the twentieth century. The artists of Mount Borradaile may have acquired Reckitt's Blue from Europeans at Palmerston (Darwin) and Pine Creek, though Baldwin Spencer felt pleased to report that it had not been used at Oenpelli in 1912. It was therefore probably introduced into western Arnhem Land by the Anglican missionaries from the 1920s. The pigment was subsequently used throughout Arnhem Land, though its use was especially prevalent around the former Oenpelli mission. Those 'blue paintings' around Mount Borradaile were probably rendered by Charlie's father's generation in the 1930s-40s. The match tin found near the Major Art habitation shelter contains some granules of Reckitt's Blue.

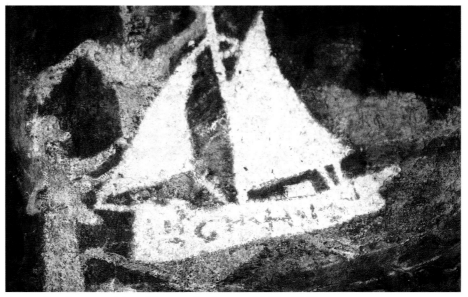

A pearling lugger with writing on the bow, c.1880s-1940s.
This is a gaff-rigged sloop, single mast, around 10 metres long. Note the box-type deck house on the counter stern.

Probably a percussion action, single shot muzzle loader, of the type used by the military and police authorities in the 1840s. We are indebted to Robert Courtney, Senior Curator of Military Heraldry and Weapons at the Australian War Memorial (Canberra), for his comments on these paintings.

A typical European-style trading ketch, c.1870s-1930s. The stern, however, is canoe-like. Ian Hansen, a sailor and keen observer of maritime vessels, was struck by the exaggerated gap between the masts and sails, suggesting the artist was illustrating the 'rat lines' or ladder-style rigging by which the sailors climbed aloft.

Steam ships, base of Mount Borradaile.

The artist demonstrates familiarity with both Macassan and European sail/steam vessels. Curiously, these figures combine characteristics of both. The top ship may have a Macassan-style rudder, but also a wheelhouse, a boiler and smokestack emitting steam.

The bottom vessel is intriguing. This is a large ship, combining sail and steam characteristics: two masts and two funnels. It may, in fact, be a British warship from the mid nineteenth century, up to 100 metres long and capable of carrying some 400 troops. The band of white on the hull, and the gunports along the side, gave those vessels a distinctive 'checker-board' look which Ian Hansen recognises in this painting. Some of the British warships of the early steam era retained sailing ship characteristics, including clipper bows and tall masts. The band of solid red ochre above the main deck may represent an awning. The artist has considerable knowledge of the workings of this vessel. He has drawn the propeller, as well as the funnel between the boiler room and stack. There appear to be figures in the gunports, drawn in black charcoal. Perhaps they are Aborigines.

A ship in sail, painted over a decorative in-fill human figure.
This is a gaff ketch, single deck, under 30 metres long. Sections of the fore-peak and hold are unshaded, presumably indicating they were empty. The mid-ship compartment which is faintly in-filled with hatched lines, may be the freshwater tank. The shaded section aft is the captain's cabin. This was probably a European pearling lugger, though the shape of the hull is characteristically Indonesian.

Beeswax Designs

Native beeswax (sugarbag) was used on occasion to decorate faces, usually in the form of pellets pressed onto the rock surface, often adorning ochre paintings such as the remarkable Beeswax Lady figure near Mount Borradaile. Beeswax pellets were

Beeswax designs in the Swimming Hole Gallery area. The wax is dark, suggesting that it has been more recently applied.

also frequently arranged in parallel lines or other patterns on the walls of habitation shelters, in the belief that this would exterminate ticks and parasites. The technique is distinctive and thought to be unique to the Arnhem Land region (Chaloupka, 1993).

In 1991, radiocarbon tests on beeswax from two simple turtle designs returned a date of about 4,000 years, though this is believed to be an uncommonly early example of the medium. Most paintings featuring beeswax pellets belong to the recent Freshwater Period and are supposed to be less than several hundred years old (Nelson et al., 1995). In the beeswax art around Mount Borradaile, the pellets have the dark, glossy texture of being recently applied. Older, more weathered fragments of beeswax are recognisably grey and brittle.

> They are very fond of honey, which appears to be in abundance, as they were seldom without a supply of that article, and when they went into the woods on purpose to procure it, they soon returned successful. Their mode of proceeding was to watch the movements of the bees (which requires a keen eye and long practice) and as soon as they saw them settle on a tree, they proceeded to cut it down, which they effected with their stone hatchets, much quicker than could be imagined.
>
> *T.B. Wilson, at Raffles Bay in 1829*

Erosion and damage (exfoliation)

The erosive elements of nature, whose effects seem so conspicuous on this ancient landscape, have obviously been the primary threat to the durability of rock art. Many paintings have been seriously damaged by water seepage, dust abrasion and mould. Native animals and insects are also a common cause of deterioration, especially termites and wasps. The introduction of buffalo to the region in the nineteenth

Wallaby and hand stencils. This type of sandstone erosion threatens many ancient art galleries in Arnhem Land and the Top End.

A long-necked turtle decorated with dots, near the Beeswax Lady gallery. The head and a segment of the body have eroded.

century posed another immediate threat to some sites. During storms, buffalo took refuge in unoccupied shelters, where they found the abrasive surfaces ideal for rubbing and scratching. In recent years, the swelling influx of non-Aborigines into the area has given rise to new hazards including, in various instances, deliberate vandalism.

THE ART OF PAINTING

Executing and maintaining a rock painting was a key part of the ambit of rituals and responsibilities vested in those responsible for particular sites — an inseparable component of the cycle of myths, songs and rituals through which Aborigines interpret, invoke and harness the powers of their physical and spiritual environment. Paintings were visual aids employed to supplement oral instruction, a critical means of sustaining knowledge, both sacred and public. In art, Aborigines relate and honour the Dreaming characters whose travels and exploits gave substance and order to the Aboriginal world. By painting and retouching, they revitalise and tether the spiritual powers associated with those mythic characters.

Rock art was, generally, the pursuit of men. In western Arnhem Land, women played key roles in the economy and religion of local Aboriginal society, though they seldom executed rock paintings. Painting skills, subject matter and clan designs were handed down patrilineally as a type of apprenticeship, with degrees of symbolism and subject matter deepening with advancing age and respective stages of initiation. Many sites and subjects relate to sacred male ritual and mythology, secreted from women and younger uninitiated males. The awe-inspiring Rainbow Serpent shelter near Mount Borradaile, for example, was identified by Big Bill Neidjie as a male

ceremonial place. Other sites/subjects were more public, as we know from the prolific and intense art galleries in larger habitation sites like the Major Art shelter near Mount Borradaile, that would have accommodated the more general population. There, among the plethora of drawings and stencils, are the simply executed designs and hand prints of small children.

We know also that various local sites are associated with 'women's business', including one near the Emu Cave that Peter Rotumah has identified, based on a distinctive painting nearby. It is unclear whether 'women's paintings' were actually executed by women, though Peter concedes that it is probable. Elsewhere, women are known to have been entrusted with the retouching of particular paintings in their capacity as senior custodians and spiritual leaders (Smith, 1991). Today, with the passing of many of the traditions associated with the area, most of the sites may now be viewed and enjoyed by all. Formerly, inappropriate viewing of certain paintings could result in sickness, accident or violent retribution as prescribed by traditional law.

The most important rock paintings are not ascribed rock to human agency. In western Arnhem Land, much of the art is attributed to the mimi. They were the 'fairy-like invisible people' whom Mountford was told were responsible for the ancient monochrome paintings around Oenpelli (Mountford, 1956). The mimi live in the crevices and caves of the escarpment and are credited with having taught Aboriginal people to paint and hunt (Carroll, 1977). As a boy, Lazarus Lamilami, on first seeing the paintings in his father's estate in the Wellington Ranges, wondered how they were executed on such high, inaccessible surfaces. He was told by older men that 'Mimi can make the top of caves come down very close. Afterward they say a magic word and blow some wind, and the paintings go back near the top of the cave. That's how the paintings are done' (Lamilami, 1974).

Particular paintings are regarded as a physiographic remnant of a mythic character. This is especially the case with depictions of powerful Dreaming Beings, which are among the most sacred local rock paintings. Such paintings are viewed as embodiments of the character, rather than a representation of it. Their existence is held as tangible evidence of the reality of that character, and proof of the associated events and myths. There were numerous traditional stories relating how beings transformed themselves into ochred paintings, such as the Mengerrdji (Oenpelli) myth of an old woman, 'Biriwilg', who made herself into a painting in order to avoid the attention of men. That particular painting was said to have fertility properties for women who visited and touched it (Berndt and Berndt, 1989). The 'Kakadu Man', Big Bill Neidjie, described many of the paintings in his clan estate as the remains or marks of specific Dreaming characters. Similarly, in Bulajang ('Sickness Country') in southern Kakadu, images of the dreaded destructor Being, Bula, are said to have been painted by Bula himself. The associated animal paintings are 'shades' of the animals hunted by Bula during his Dreaming travels. Nearby female figures were 'shades' of women killed by Bula for trespassing in secret male sites (Gunn, 1992).

As a visual aid employed to supplement oral instruction, animal and fish paintings, particularly the X-ray designs which divulge an incisive anatomical knowledge, could have been particularly useful for teaching young men how to hunt, prepare and distribute a catch. Such paintings could also be read as 'maps' in which anatomical details were construed to represent geographical features, plotting favorable sites for

The haematite figure holding a club in his right hand is painted with broad, relatively indelicate strokes. Aborigines might describe it as a 'rubbish painting'. It is superimposed over the head of the white pipe-clay figure on the left, giving the appearance of a fight or assault.

hunting and fishing (Tacon, 1988). Some fauna paintings may have pertained to forms of 'hunting magic', reflecting strategies intended to ensure the successful pursuit of game. Throughout the region there are well documented 'increase sites' and associated paintings which relate to particular faunal and floral species. At Ubirr in Kakadu National Park, Aborigines were said to have lightly struck a water-snake painting with branches to animate the water-snake spirit, in order to fill the waterholes with large water-snakes (Mountford, 1956). More recent inquiries suggest that relatively few paintings were actually related to hunting magic, though some animal and fish paintings were produced or retouched after a hunt, sometimes in response to failure to procure food (Tacon, 1988).

While much of the art was a product of religious and mythological concerns, sometimes encapsulating the most confidential and sacred knowledge, artists also painted for pleasure, depicting subjects that were of casual or personal interest. Some paintings may reflect personal stories or experiences, relating specific events such as a notable hunting expedition or the sighting of balanda. In more recent times, the disruption and deterioration of old cultural and artistic traditions wrought by European invasion fostered a phase of informal, desultory rock paintings, executed haphazardly and inexpertly by untrained artists. Scholars call this 'casual art', though Aborigines refer to them less charitably as 'rubbish' paintings (Chaloupka, 1993).

Food and Sex

The principal subjects in the rock paintings around Mount Borradaile are of the various faunal species that formed the staple of the Aboriginal diet, and females — food and sex being 'the two most important aspects in the social life of the human being' (Berndt and Berndt, 1951). Most of the fauna paintings are of aquatic species. Fish paintings are especially prevalent in the northern parts of western Arnhem Land,

Kangaroo-headed Being.
This therianthropic character, with its anthropomorphic body and kangaroo head, is depicted elsewhere in the East Alligator River region in ochre and beeswax. It is a product of the recent, Freshwater Period and is known to embody a powerful mythic Being. (Tacon, pers.com).

reflecting the fecundity of the rivers, lagoons and wetlands. Further south, inland towards the higher, rocky country, macropod paintings predominate. Aquatic species like barramundi and catfish also feature prominently in the traditional belief systems of this area (Tacon, 1993).

There is an 'apparent preoccupation' with female features in much of the rock art of northern Australia, intimating the importance of women's sexual role in Aboriginal society (Bullen, 1991). Early observers of western Arnhem Land culture were particularly struck by a conspicuous degree of 'eroticism' in local mythology and ritual. It mirrored a heightened understanding of 'the fecundity of the female, with her powers of generation, embodying the increase of the human and natural species' (Berndt and Berndt, 1951). This eroticism is clearly exhibited in the rock art around Mount Borradaile, where females and female genitalia are the predominant subject — and the most singular aspect — of the Recent Period paintings. The paintings are, in short, manifestations of a spirituality centered on abstractions of fertility, reproduction and renewal.

These abstractions are epitomised by the centrality in regional mythology of powerful female Beings, including the principal Dreaming character,

Warramurrunggundji, the 'First Mother' whose acts of Creation are central to the major ritual sequences of western Arnhem Land. Throughout the region, the Mother is embodied in a myriad of legends and rituals concerning two women (usually sisters), most famously the Wawalag Sisters of northern Arnhem Land, the Djanggawul Sisters of the north-east, and the Yawk Yawk Sisters of the Kunwinjku-speaking clans. Sisters are clearly evident in some recent paintings in the Mount Borradaile region, as in the Mangulda gallery.

There are also various recorded traditions among the old cultures of the East Alligator River region respecting the sexual relations between women and spirit Beings. The 'best known' example, first recorded in 1940s, related the exploits of Aranga the 'green ant', a malevolent spirit with an abnormally large penis, whose likeness was painted in a shelter above Inyaluk lagoon (Oenpelli). The legend associated with this painting concerned two Amurdak sisters who, lost in the bush, entered Aranga's camp. Thinking Aranga was human they consented to sex, which left them sore and bleeding. In retribution, Aboriginal men dug a large pit and lured Aranga into it, where he was beaten, speared and buried. But Aranga survived, and was later heard playing his penis like a didjeridu. This event was credited as the origin of the instrument. An equivalent version of the Aranga tradition was told and painted on bark by a Kunwinjku artist at Oenpelli in 1947 (Berndt and Berndt, 1951; Berndt, Berndt and Stanton, 1992) and it bears close similarity to the contemporary Kunwinjku story of Bilk Bilk, recorded by Adrian Parker in 1996 (Parker, 1997).

Many of the local paintings in fact combine female-human and animal characteristics. The human figures of the Recent Period are mostly therianthropic, combining human with kangaroo, fish and snake features. These would relate mostly to Dreaming characters associated with particular species. The long, lithe bodies of the Full Figure humans are distinctly serpent-like. We may also perceive insect-like characteristics in the human figures, reflective of the importance in regional mythology of insects such as the grasshopper (Grove, 1999).

The relationship between human and animal motifs is also apparent on other levels. In some panels there are evident relationships between two or more separate works, either painted contiguously or with one superimposed over another (older) painting. Around Mount Borradaile there is an apparent association between female human figures and fish, which appear together at various sites. The fish is often a fork-tailed (Arius leptaspis) or eel-tailed (Tandanus tandanus) catfish. An American scholar, Peggy Grove, who has researched the iconography and mythology of the Mount Borradaile region, proposes that these motifs are also related by a number of shared characteristics. There are, for example, resemblances between the 'corpulent vulva' design in female figures, the tail or mouth of some fish and the mouth of some snake or Rainbow Serpent paintings (Grove, 1999). Recent Period human and fauna paintings also commonly feature what appear to be antlers or horns protruding from the neck or head, possibly insect-like antenna or the barbs of the catfish or stingray. These protrusions may also reference the 'horns' of the Rainbow Serpent, as described in the oral traditions recorded at Oenpelli in the 1950s (see below). Women, serpents and fish are potent symbols of fertility and renewal in western Arnhem Land. The similarities and associations in the rock art may express natural and metaphorical analogies between these symbols in Aboriginal cosmology. As such they probably relate to mythology and rituals concerning Warramurrunggundji, the

Female figure, Emu Cave, near Mount Borradaile
A multitude of Recent Period female figures are found in this corner of the Mount Borradaile region. This is one of the more fascinating examples. Note the thin, mantis-like body, and the flat, blunt head with antennae-like protrusions. This is one of numerous illustrations of women holding 'strings' above their head, probably a cat's cradle, used by performers in the kunapipi and ubarr rituals.

Disassociated paintings of female vulva, near Mount Borradaile. The larger painting on the bottom right illustrates a penis.

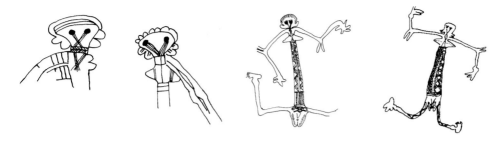

The Full Figure paintings of the Recent Period combine human and animal characteristics. The anthropomorphic frames are mantis-like, with their elongated, contorted body parts. The flat, blunt head of many figures may mimic the large, bright grasshopper Valanga irregularis, abundant in northern Australia. Many human figures, and some animal paintings, feature antenna-like protrusions from the head, which are also suggestive of insect characteristics (Grove, 1999).

A Recent Period painting near the Cooper Creek Lightning Man. This is probably a barramundi, judging by the spiky spines of the dorsal fin, though the design of the mouth is unusual, reminiscent of the 'corpulent vulva' design of many Recent Period human figures (Grove, 1999).

Rainbow Serpent and kunapipi. It should be noted, however, that such theories are rarely sustained by discussions with contemporary Aboriginal elders, who are usually inimical to balanda's attempts to interpret and rationalise their culture. For Peter Rotumah the catfish is a 'sacred emblem' and he will not discuss it.

Associated fish and female figures, near Mount Borradaile. These are beautiful examples of Full Figure paintings from the Recent/Freshwater Period. The rock paintings around Mount Borradaile are predominantly individual works, rather than multi-figure compositions. There are, for instance, no 'scenes' comparable to the evocative 'conflict paintings' found in the Magela Creek — Cannon Hill area. However, as elsewhere, individual paintings often appear in association with others. This panel is one of a number around Mount Borradaile in which representations of female human figures and fish appear together. The meaning of this association is unknown.

Associated female and fish paintings, near the Beeswax Lady. The female figure with the 'yawning mouth' and long, writhing arm and five fingers, is the older painting. The solid white in-fill and cross-hatching are fading. The fish painting represents a sleepy cod (Oxyeleotris lineolatus), using native beeswax for eyes. Its tail-end is reminiscent of the 'corpulent vulva' design (Grove, 1999). Combined, the paintings give the appearance of a fish swallowing a female Being.

Love Magic and Sorcery Paintings

The so-called sorcery paintings are those executed with the intention of cursing and harming an individual. For those vested with the necessary powers, painting was one of various means of working sorcery. Lazarus Lamilami, who grew up on Goulburn Island, recalled that it was the speciality of the mainland people. 'They knew about singing ... they could sing someone to die' (Lamilami, 1974). Sorcery intentions might be detected in some human figures which are depicted in painfully contorted postures, with twisted limbs, deformed fingers or grossly swollen joints. Elsewhere in the region, human figures have been painted with severed limbs, or with their bodies pierced by spears, possibly indicating sorcery at work. Sorcery paintings are thought to have become most emphasised during the contact era. They are most commonly found in this corner of Arnhem Land where contact with outsiders was most prolonged and extensive, and most damaging.

Analogous to the sorcery paintings were those associated with 'love magic'. The art of love magic in Arnhem Land was described by Ronald and Catherine Berndt, who observed it at a time when the techniques were still practised on rock and bark, but when their use was declining (Berndt and Berndt, 1951). Love magic may underscore some paintings depicting copulation, executed with the intention of seducing an otherwise unwilling female. They might be repainted or retouched to reinvigorate the charm, if the first attempt is fruitless. Other paintings endeavoured to induce pregnancy, depicting a pregnant woman with foetus or a women breastfeeding. The Berndts identified love magic in Oenpelli rock paintings of women with child attached by umbilical cord. There is one exquisite example of this outside the Emu Cave near Mount Borradaile.

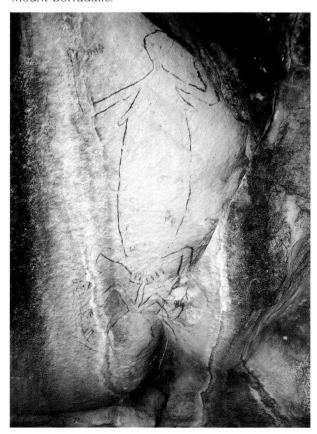

Outside the Emu Cave is this unusual painting of a female giving birth, measuring 1.5 metres in length. The baby is still attached via the umbilical cord. This is a 'women's painting' according to Peter Rotumah, and marks a site formerly associated with secret female ritual.

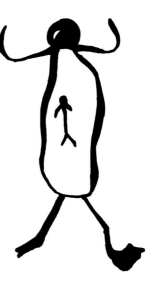

A simple painting near the Cooper Creek Lightning Man shelter, apparently representing a pregnant figure, though the gender is not otherwise indicated.

Ochres and brushes

Ochres are obtained from various ores and clays, found mostly in the vicinity of waterways, washouts and coastal areas. Red ochre (haematite/iron ore) produces various shades of red, some of them slightly purply or brown. Yellow ochres (limonite/iron oxide) range from deep yellow to brown, and when burnt may form a purply red. White is obtained from various clays. Some paintings in the Mount Borradaile region, including the astonishing Rainbow Serpent, were made using the ochre of compressed silt, acquired nearby. Black pigment is obtained from ground charcoal or manganese ore, though it features less frequently in the rock paintings of western Arnhem Land than in the east.

Ochre has always been an important item of Aboriginal trade. The extraction and acquisition of ochre was a deeply significant event, and the sites from which it was obtained were of great spiritual importance. One of the several major trade ceremonies of western Arnhem Land, the Njalaidj, revolved around the acquisition of red ochre from the south. Ronald Berndt, who observed the Njalaidj at Oenpelli in the late 1940s, thought it the most spectacular of the regional trade ceremonies, resembling 'the beautiful sacred dancing' of the kunapipi rituals (Berndt, 1974).

Aside from rock surfaces, ochre was also applied to tools, especially sacred ceremonial objects, and to bodies. Hunters adorned themselves as a means of camouflage and to reduce body odour, while performers were decorated in singular and sacred designs to animate dance and song. Ochre was also used to ornament bones during burial ceremonies. In 1967, fragments of a human skull painted with red ochre was found at PadyPadiy, west of the East Alligator River near Jabiru (White, 1967). A number of painted skulls and bones have also been found in the Mount Borradaile region.

Archaeological excavations of rock-shelters in the region have uncovered many small pieces of haematite worn in a manner suggesting they were used as crayons on the rock surface. Generally, however, pigments were prepared by grinding or pounding lumps of ochre into a powder form, perhaps using a rock and grinding hole in the manner of a mortar and pestle, with water added to liquefy the pigment. Softer ochres could be soaked and mashed in vessels made of paperbark.

Red ochre, when ground into pigment, breaks down into much finer particles than other ochres. Like the paint in many wet frescoes, painted millenniums ago by European cultures, haematite is often absorbed into the painting surface. There it bonds with the silica of the rock, staining the sandstone and resisting erosion. The other colours, yellow, black and (especially) white, do not grind so finely and are subsequently more resistant to absorption and more susceptible to erosion. Numerous natural additives can be used as bonding agents to make the painting more adhesive and resilient to rubbing or flaking. They included egg white, plant saps, bodily fluids and animal blood.

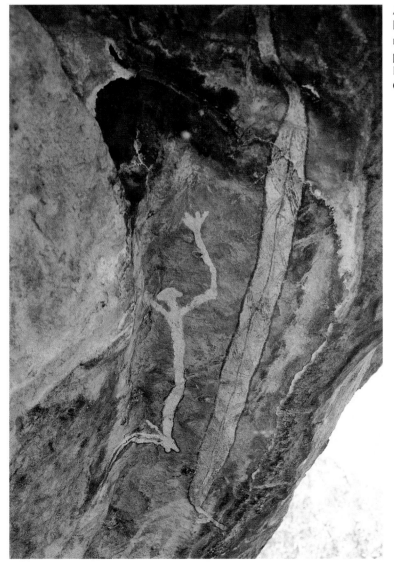

A mushroom-headed human male figure and a python, near Jabiru Rock, lower Cooper Creek.

THE GALLERIES OF THE MOUNT BORRADAILE REGION

Chapter 5

MANGULDA GALLERY

The Mangulda Gallery is one of numerous art sites located around the base of Mount Borradaile; one of the few in that area we are allowed to view. This gallery was named after Charlie Mangulda's father. Charlie recalls him painting here, possibly in the 1940s. Those paintings were probably the last to be executed in the Cooper Creek region.

The paintings in this area include a number of coupled female figures, or 'sisters', suggestive of the Two Sisters element in the Aboriginal belief systems of northern Australia. The Sisters were pivotal creation/fertility figures who defined languages, designated estates and instituted the customs by which bininj live. In northern and eastern Arnhem Land there are the Wawalag Sisters who were swallowed by Yulunggul the rock python (sometimes a Rainbow Serpent) after one of the Sisters allowed her afterbirth to foul a waterhole. The Wawalag mythology is central to the kunapipi rituals, which are concerned with fertility, reproduction and renewal. The Wawalag Sisters was a 'transition myth between the cultures of western and eastern Arnhem Land' (Berndt, 1970) and may not have penetrated the Borradaile region, except in very recent times. Among the traditional cultures of western Arnhem Land, the 'First Mother' or 'Fertility Mother', Warramurrunggundji, is sometimes articulated as two women (Berndt and Berndt, 1951 & 1970; Welch, 1992; Chaloupka, 1993).

Mangulda rock-shelter and gallery, Mount Borradaile, named after Charlie's father, who was the last to add his work to this complex mosaic of figurative paintings.

The 'Two Sisters'. These recent female figure paintings are highlighted by intricate hatching on a white ochre base. The right arm appears to be severed. 'This is sacred, secret story' according to the Amurdak elder, Peter Rotumah.

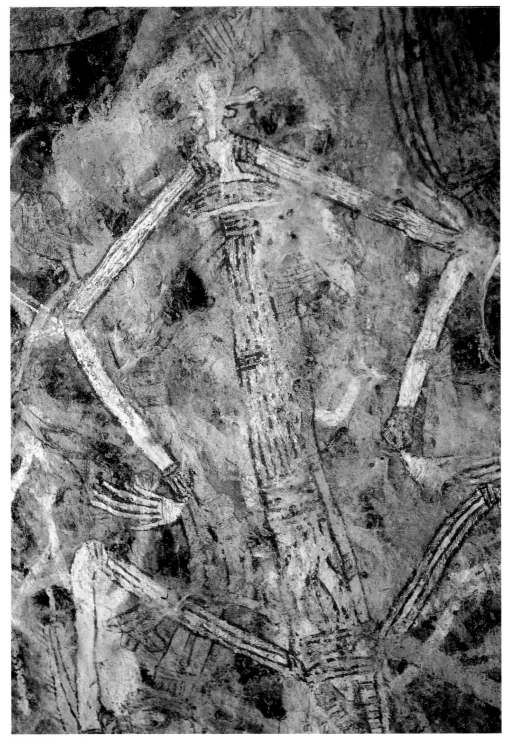

An exquisite Full Figure female painting, with decorative in-fill on a white background. Note the long, supple fingers and the antennae-like protrusions from the head.

The astonishing Mount Borradaile Rainbow Serpent. George Chaloupka identified this Serpent as Aburga, painted within the last 1,500 years by an artist of the Amurdak language group.

THE MOUNT BORRADAILE RAINBOW SERPENT

The Rainbow Serpent is recognised as the world's oldest surviving religious theme. It is thought to have emerged along the changing coastal areas of Arnhem Land during the Pleistocene-Holocene transition period, over 6,000 years ago. The earliest Serpent paintings in this region coincide with the art of the Yam period. They are small, composite figures: snakes with macropod-heads, spiked tails and yam and water-lily appendages trailing from the body. Close analysis of these images suggests they were derived from the skeletons of tiny sea horses or the Ribboned pipefish, washed up on beaches and banks during the period of rising sea-levels. Like numerous local aquatic species, male pipefish incubate and hatch eggs in their mouths, releasing their offspring in a manner suggestive of the regurgitation/regeneration theme in modern Rainbow Serpent mythology (Tacon, Wilson and Chippindale, 1996). Recent Rainbow Serpent rock paintings are larger illustrations; fearsome creatures painted in the decorative in-fill style, commonly represented with crocodile, kangaroo or human features. To Aborigines, they are among the most potent and profound of all rock paintings.

Among the first Rainbow Serpent stories recorded by anthropologists was one told to Professor Baldwin Spencer at Oenpelli in 1912. Spencer's Gagadju informants named the Serpent 'Numereji', illustrated in one of the bark paintings he collected (now held in the National Museum of Victoria). As the story was told to Spencer, Numereji first appeared on a plain between the East Alligator River and Cooper Creek, where it was disturbed by the sound of a screaming child. The theme of the crying child — usually a child demanding a foodstuff or object that is sacred or forbidden — was a common element in the regional Rainbow Serpent myths recorded by anthropologists throughout the twentieth century (see, for example, Berndt and Berndt, 1970 and 1989). Numereji swallowed the child and pursued its family, devouring them with his tongue. Numereji then moved down the East Alligator River, where it attempted to creep up on another party of people. They were alerted when Numereji frightened a flock of white cranes and cockatoos. Numereji then rose high in the air and vomited the bones of the men and women he had eaten, before departing to the place where he remained asleep in the ground (Spencer, 1928).

In Amurdak, the Rainbow Serpent is Aburga. Among the Kunwinjku, he is Ngalyod, though the Kunwinjku First Mother, Yingarna, is also usually identified as a Serpent. (Yingarna and Ngalyod are famously represented in modern Oenpelli bark paintings). In its various guises, the Rainbow Serpents of western Arnhem Land originated from the sea and reside presently in rivers, waterholes and rocks. They are associated with the procreative and regenerative forces of nature, and are central to the major fertility and initiatory ceremonies such as kunapipi, ubarr and yaburdurwa. In western Arnhem Land mythology, Serpents are commonly agents of retribution and destruction. The appearance of a Rainbow Serpent can be a 'fear-inspiring and punitive' moment (Berndt and Berndt, 1970). They were often described as having horns or stingray nails protruding from the head, and could emit a stunning light from the eyes. People were alerted to the approach of Rainbow Serpents by the crashing and cracking of trees, and by the howling wind, roaring 'like the combined voices of many bees, or like a huge bush-fire speeding towards them' (Berndt and Berndt, 1989). In a Maung tradition, when the Serpent Ambidj appeared off the coast of Goulburn Island, the people heard thunderous waves and saw flames out to sea (Lamilami, 1974).

George Chaloupka has identified the Mount Borradaile Rainbow Serpent painting as belonging to the now extinct Amurdak-speaking Malakiri clan (Hulley, 1999). Painted in white ochre and haematite, it is the largest known Rainbow Serpent painting in Australia, measuring 6.1 metres (20 feet) in length, with almost a metre between the tips of the gaping jaws. Its main features are the fearsome teeth

The gaping jaws of Aburga.

protruding from a dragon like head, and the tongue, which was a key element of the Serpent, Numereji, described to Spencer in 1912. The sinuous body of the Serpent features a type of flipper or fin. Note the fine detail of the spine and rib structure. The protrusions behind the head — the 'horns' or 'collar' — are suggestive of myths told to Ronald Berndt concerning a boy, Gurulmulya, who was accosted by a Rainbow Serpent while collecting lily stalks from a billabong in Amurdak country. Gurulmulya climbed onto the cold, slippery back of the Serpent, gripping the stingray nails behind its head, and rode it up and down Cooper Creek through the night. Gurulmulya died the next day when he washed off the smelly goo. Bininj people were cautioned not to collect lilies at that billabong (Berndt and Berndt, 1989).

This is a dry, accessible shelter with no signs of habitation, indicating that it was strictly a ceremonial site. There are various habitations shelters in the immediate vicinity. In this particular shelter there is very little art other than the main image, and there have been no images superimposed over any part of it. Clearly, this is testimony to the importance of this painting.

An unidentified symbol, or possibly an unfinished painting, one of the few other paintings on the wall of the Rainbow Serpent shelter.

MAJOR ART

Major Art is one of the larger and more accessible shelters of the Mount Borradaile region, lying on the brim of the vast Cooper Creek wetlands near Davidson's Safari camp. This was undoubtedly a primary habitation site. Spacious and well protected, it could accommodate large congregations at the height of the Wet Season. Today it still wears the appearance of having being recently vacated. Grinding stones, spear tips, crockery and chiselled glass lie where they were left. Soot from campfires has stained the right-hand side of the shelter. The surrounding scrub contains a wide variety of foods, herbs, medicines and materials.

This is one of the most breathtaking and intense art galleries in the entire region. The wall is covered in vibrant earth reds, yellows and white, painted layer atop layer, depicting hundreds of subjects compiled over many generations. The most immediately striking feature is the abundance of hand-stencils, the signatures of the shelter's inhabitants. There is a wealth of figurative and religious paintings. This gallery also contains some of the region's most exciting contact art, including illustrations of a sailing ship and a number of rifles and pistols (discussed in an earlier section on the Contact Period). The assorted ochre colours and hues are sharply contrasted by the use of Reckitt's Blue, the bleaching agent introduced by Europeans early in the twentieth century.

A section of the wall at Major Art. On the ledge in the foreground are two grinding holes and a grinding stone.

A section of the wall at Major Art. An old tin whistle was found
nestled on the ledge in the lower-centre of the picture.

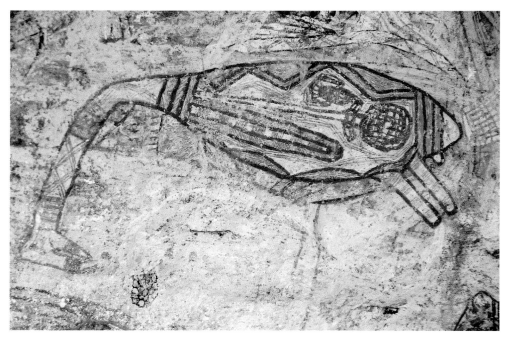

A decorative X-ray painting of a male magpie goose (Anseranus semipalmatta).
Aboriginal informants stipulate that the dots clustered near the bird's mouth represent the
bird 'speaking'. Magpie geese are abundant on the wetlands and a popular subject in the
art of the Freshwater Period. The geese nest on the flooded lowlands after the monsoons.
The eggs are relished by Aboriginal people. Months later, when the geese are fattened
and huddled together on the contracting billabongs, they are a prize catch. They were
generally hunted with sticks, spears and poles, though Lazarus Lamilami recalls a more
elaborate technique employed by his father, who constructed mud shelters on the edges
of billabongs. He used lily roots to bait the geese, grabbing them by the feet as they
descended on the shelter (Lamilami, 1974).

The identity and significance of these unusual figures is unknown, though they are doubtlessly mythical Beings of some description, probably with insect characteristics (Tacon, pers.com). They appear to be wearing collared robes and hats. The body joints and genitals are abnormally swollen. Some observers have speculated that they are Europeans, possibly missionaries, or perhaps Chinamen, who have a long association with the East Alligator River region. There were Chinese miners at Pine Creek and loggers on Barron Island near the mouth of the East Alligator River in the late nineteenth century. The long yellow painting protruding from the right is the tail of a saltwater crocodile, superimposed over the white figures. Hand stencils put their size in perspective.

'Dancing figures'.
These animated figures are stylistically similar to others found in the renowned galleries at Nourlangie Rock, which are among the most region's most recent paintings. Here they are strongly emboldened by the use of haematite pigment over a chalky, white sandstone background. The rarrk pattern in-fill appears to have remained unfinished.

Decorated hand-stencils, two with Reckitt's Blue. The stencil on the left appears to have a sleeve at its base.

The exact species of this fish cannot be identified, though it is probably a fork-tailed (Arius graeffei) or salmon catfish (Arius leptaspis). Catfish are abundant in local rivers and billabongs and are a favoured delicacy of the Aboriginal diet. The male incubates and hatches eggs in its mouth. This figure exhibits the same type of antenna-like protrusions that are characteristic of Recent Period female figures, reminiscent also of the 'horns' of the Mount Borradaile Rainbow Serpent painting.

ARTEFACT CAVE

Located near the Major Art habitation site, the Artefact Cave is named after the vast array of items found scattered on the floors of the shelters, and particularly after a cache of articles stashed in a crevice, which includes objects from the Contact Period. The area contains some of the finest local examples of decorative in-fill painting, as well as haematite figures in the Dynamic style, including another rare depiction of the boomerang. The predominant subject in this area is the female figure, many featuring tassels on the elbows and ankles. According to Big Bill Neidjie, the tassels, made of grass, indicate that the woman was a widow. They were removed by her family after a two year mourning period.

Magpie goose in X-ray style, painted over a fish and hand stencil.

A female figure. The protrusions from the elbow have been identified by Aboriginal informants as 'mourning tassels', worn by a widow. A widow is not allowed to take another man or speak her deceased husband's name for a specified period. At the figure's left is a hand stencil in which the forefinger and midfinger have been placed together.

A rock wallaby enclosed in a 'frame'.

In 1912, Baldwin Spencer described a tradition among 'Kakadu' men regarding three snakes, 'Kuljoango' and 'Jeluabi', who were described as non-venomous, and 'Ngabadaua', 'a special one' who was regarded as the 'head of all the snake groups'. Ngabadaua was said to figure prominently in the traditions of the Kakadu. In a dance witnessed by Spencer at Oenpelli, Ngabadaua was represented as 'a quick-moving, vicious animal of which the natives are very much afraid'. In the dance, men representing various snakes come to look for Ngabadua in order to kill him. Kuljoango and Jeluabi are persuaded to take them to Ngabadau's home, were Ngabadaua discovers them and kills them (Spencer, 1928).

The snakes have been painted over and around two excellent Dynamic Figures with spears, boomerangs and headdress. These are impeccable examples of one of the oldest forms of human-figure paintings, executed in the Pre-Estuarine era, over 10,000 years ago.

EMU CAVE

The Emu Cave is so named because of a beautiful painting of an emu (Dromaius novaehollandiae) sitting on a clutch of six eggs. This shelter contains some of the finest examples of Recent Period art, including paintings of freshwater aquatic species and several, outstanding female full-figure paintings.

The Emu Cave.

The Emu.
Emus were hunted for food, and their feathers used for ceremonial headdresses, though they have been virtually eradicated from Arnhem Land and Kakadu. This painting is distinguishable by the unique shape of its feet and wings. The emu is sitting on a clutch of six eggs. Bunidj clansmen have indicated that the dots painted near its mouth symbolise the bird 'speaking'. This painting, including the eggs, is roughly 180 cm in height.

Spirit Figure, Emu Cave.
This unique painting, with its elongated legs and arms, and elbows attached to the hips, measures 2.1 metres in length. George Chaloupka has identified this as a malignant Namorrodo spirit who steals the soul of the dying (Chaloupka, 1993). However, it is also very suggestive of the Dreaming character described by Baldwin Spencer as 'Wuraka' (Wurragag), the partner of Warramurrunggundji (the 'First Mother'). Wurragag was said to have come from the north-west, walking through the sea. 'His feet were on the bottom, but he was so tall that his head was well above water'. Wurragag's enormous penis, which he carried over his shoulder, was so heavy that he retired from his Dreaming travels and rested at the site now marked by Tor Rock, 20 kilometres north of Mount Borradaile (Spencer, 1928). In Kunwinjku legend, Wurragag brought fire to the mainland and taught Aboriginal people to cook meat. He transformed himself into Tor Rock in order to avoid the vengeance of Amurdak clansmen, after taking a wife who had already been betrothed (Berndt and Berndt, 1970). Big Bill Neidjie, in conversations with Max Davidson, confirmed that this painting evoked a story of a Being who walked through the ocean.

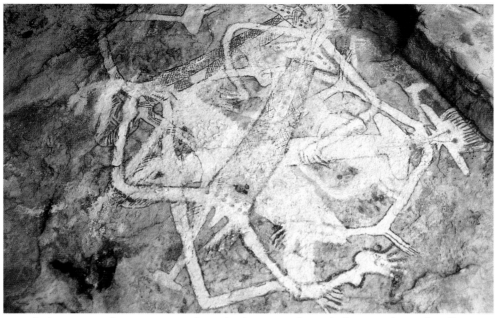

Female figures overlaying one another. The figure on the right has tassels on the elbows, while other figures have dotted breasts. The central figure had dots along the torso and across the waist.

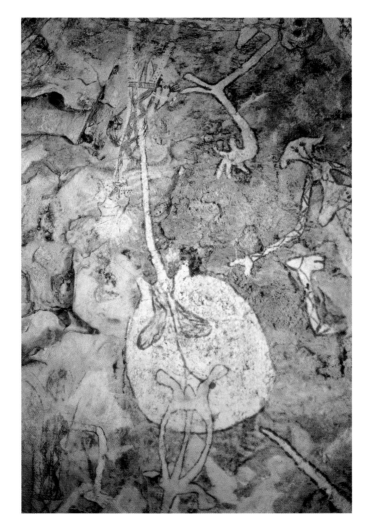

A stingray with the X-ray features. This illustration highlights the eyes, and the liver, which was used for oil. The raw liver was removed from the stingray before cooking and the oil was extracted. The residue of the liver was then mixed with the cooked stingray and consumed.

PAPERBARK BEDS

The Paperbark Beds shelter and associated galleries lie a short distance from the Mount Borradaile Rainbow Serpent. The cave is one of the most fascinating habitation shelters in the region, providing rare and unique evidence of both ancient and recent Aboriginal occupation.

The structures are made from paperbark beams harvested from the nearby swamps. They are erected to form a platform over which sheets of paperbark are strewn to make a bed. Smouldering clumps of termite nest were placed underneath to repel mosquitoes, in the manner of a modern mosquito coil. Another, more recently introduced repellant was smouldering buffalo manure. These paperbark beds are thought to have been built around 50 years ago, when a group of Aboriginal men lived here briefly at the behest of the Oenpelli missionaries. The beams have been cut with a steel axe.

Outside the cave, there are a number of galleries and isolated paintings which are predominately in the older styles of local rock art, including classic examples of Dynamic and naturalistic faunal figures. There has been little recent painting over the older art in this area, or the more recent paintings have been washed away, as most of these galleries are fairly exposed. Of particular note are the peculiar human figures in headdress. There are also several boomerang stencils, one of the most famous instruments of Australian Aboriginal society. Once used for hunting and fighting, the boomerang is featured throughout Arnhem Land in paintings associated with the Dynamic style, though they have not been used in the region (except as clapsticks) for about 4,000 years, since the emerging woodland environment made them ineffective (Flood, 1997).

The Paperbark Beds habitation shelter.

'The kitchen' at the Paperbark Beds. Grindstones rest in the holes where native grasses, seeds and foodstuffs were prepared.

Layers of naturalistic fauna, human figure paintings and hand stencils. They include depictions of the short-eared rock wallaby, and a human figure in the Dynamic style, holding a large multi-barbed spear.

A long-necked turtle (Chelodina rugosa), 60 cm long.
Long-necked turtles were gathered in the Cooper Creek wetlands and were a popular food. This image is threatened by erosion. To its left are the faded remnants of old hand stencils.

Bulbous-headed dancing figures. These highly peculiar figures, about 20 cm in height, are wearing headdresses and appear to be dancing in line. They probably belong to Chaloupka's Post-Dynamic Figure category (Tacon, pers.com), predating the Simple Figures of the Estuarine Period. Possibly older than 6,000 years of age, they are threatened by local erosion to the rock face. On the lower right-hand side is a painting of an eel-tailed catfish.

Short-eared rock wallaby, distinguished by its curled tail with brushy end. More recent art painted with pipe-clay has eroded to reveal this older haematite painting.

Boomerang and hand stencils.
Boomerangs are widely depicted in stencils and paintings throughout the region.
They are particularly associated with the styles of the Pre-Estuarine Period, when the
boomerang was an availing weapon for hunting on the expansive grasslands. The
emergence of extensive forests and woodlands during the Estuarine Period
diminished the value of the boomerang, and they have not been used in the region
for about 4,000 years.

Dynamic Figure with boomerang.

To the right of this female figure, dozens of layers of art have been painted, one over the other. Human figures, birds and other animals are the primary subjects.

Contorted figures
These two male figures are badly twisted into uncomfortable positions. They have unusual swellings on their right arms, suggesting possible broken limbs and/or sorcery at work. Peter Rotumah, an Amurdak elder, identified these as 'rock spirits'.

BEESWAX LADY

The walk to the Beeswax Lady proceeds from the Lightning Man site, past numerous habitation and art sites. The Beeswax Lady is the main feature of a gallery on the underside of a large rock, atop a stony ridge with panoramic views.

The large, precariously balanced rock under which the Beeswax Lady and other works of art have been painted. The soot suggests that this was an occasional living area. A grindstone hole lies in the left hand foreground.

The Beeswax Lady (72 cm from head to knees).
This female figure is of the recent Freshwater Period. A white background (possibly a much older painting) has been in-filled from neck to knee with fine strokes. The painting is adorned with 14 small pellets of beeswax, placed at the eyes, neck, nipples, elbows, wrists, hips, vagina and knees.

Female figure and catfish. The double string connecting her hands has been identified as a cat's cradle. String figures were woven to depict stories and themes. The figure has been painted over a series of jabirus (bottom centre). Jabirus have inhabited the region since the onset of the Freshwater Period, so the female figure is a relatively recent painting. To the left of this figure is a painting of an eel-tailed catfish.

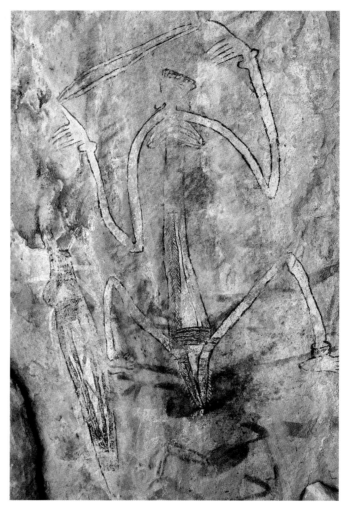

Some of the art to be found approaching Beeswax Lady. This painting contains longtoms (or 'needlefish'), a catfish and human forms.

A three-fingered female figure, painted over an earlier painting of a catfish.

BROLGA CAMP

The Brolga Camp habitation sites and galleries are named because of the large Brolga population that lives nearby. Like the other galleries that surround the Cooper Creek wetlands, Brolga camp contains a great diversity of styles and subjects, from grass and hand prints characteristic of the Pre-Estuarine Period, to decorative in-fill figures and stencils that have been painted in the last few hundred years.

Human figures, monitor lizards and foot stencils. The human figures have exaggerated genitalia and upstanding hair (possibly headdresses).

Female forms, Brolga Camp.

JABIRU ROCK

A short drive west of Brolga Camp lies Jabiru Rock, on the vast Cooper Creek wetlands as they approach the East Alligator River flood plain. The concave, oval shaped belly of the rock accommodates a number of well preserved ochre images. The gallery is dominated by two large paintings, one of a fish, and an older, circular figure appearing 'in a study' on the top left of the gallery. They are surrounded by a collection of anthropomorphic and therianthropic figures. One larger figure has a kangaroo or hooked head with unusual protrusions, possibly insect-like antennae (as in other Recent Period paintings), though they most resemble buffalo horns. Wild buffalo spread south from the Cobourg Peninsula during the era of the early British settlements.

The precariously balanced Jabiru Rock. Note the clearly defined drip-line.

Paintings on the underbelly of Jabiru Rock. The subject of the main circular figure, which appears elsewhere in the Mount Borradaile region, is unknown.

Buffalo-headed human figure, clearly male. The other figure on the left-hand side has a rounded, kangaroo-like torso with legs severed at the knees.

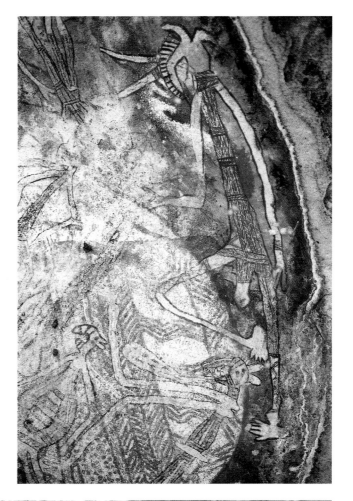

Recent Period paintings, Jabiru Rock.
The bottom section of the gallery at Jabiru Rock contains various small anthropomorphic figures with male genitalia. The figure on the right has a mouth similar to that of a dog or dingo, and wears a large erection.

The Buffalo Gallery. The decorative X-ray figures are painted over much earlier styles and works. Fish, human forms and a monitor are immediately visible. To the lower left lies the enormous yellow head and mouth of a Rainbow Serpent. The Serpent appears to have a limp human figure in its jaws, possibly added at a later date. To the upper left lie two parallel sets of beeswax dotted lines.

THE SWIMMING HOLE

A short walk from the Cooper Creek swimming hole there are a collection of galleries and burial sites referred to as the Swimming Hole shelters. One major site, labelled the Buffalo Gallery after a buffalo horn and horse shoe found nearby, contains an abundance of decorative in-fill figures that exemplify the style of the Freshwater Period.

A second gallery some 100 metres away, features some very striking human forms, including one holding a spear-thrower and hunting spears, and representations of women lactating.

The Second Swimming Hole gallery. The two women appear to be lactating. Closer inspection reveals the body of a Rainbow Serpent with small human figures in its belly. Typically, the Rainbow Serpent swallows its victims, as in the stories pertaining to the 'crying child'. In some traditions the First Mother, Warramurrunggundji (or Yingarna among the Kunwinjku), is described as a Rainbow Serpent. She held all the original ancestors in her belly, disgorging them after she was speared.

Reclining figure holding a goose-wing fan, spear thrower or fighting pick, and hunting spears. The fan was made from bunched goose-feathers, and used for swatting flies and fanning embers. An unusual design, possibly representing a garment, decorates the lower torso.

An unusually shaped female figure who appears to be expressing milk from her left breast. The right leg has been bent double. This motif appears in several places in this immediate area. On the left is the lower portion of a similar figure. Faint remnants of other paintings are also visible.

THYLACINE CAVE

In the escarpment near the Rainbow Serpent gallery, lies the Thylacine Cave. The shelter is high in the cliffs, accessible only by a steep climb through an entanglement of rocks and narrow pathways. There are two thylacine paintings in this shelter, unmistakably represented by the dark stripes along the back and the long, thin, tapered hind end. The thylacine, or Tasmanian Tiger (Thylacinus cynocephalus) was Australia's largest carnivorous marsupial. By the time Europeans arrived, the thylacine was extinct on the mainland and only resident on Tasmania. Thousands were slaughtered late in the nineteenth century after the Tasmanian government offered a £1 bounty for adult thylacines. The last thylacine died in a Hobart zoo in 1936. Rock paintings in the western Arnhem Land region attest to Aboriginal familiarity with the creature. To date, over 60 thylacine paintings have been found in western Arnhem Land, including some on the Upper East Alligator River, at Deaf Adder Creek, and further west along the Cadell River (Brandl, 1972; Chaloupka, 1993).

The thylacine, 140 cm in length, plus renderings of wallabies. The lower part of the rock face is seriously eroded.

A large figure in bold, white ochre, probably a barramundi. To the right is a faint outline of a second thylacine painting.

A dugong, 110 cm in length.
The dugong or 'sea cow' is an aquatic herbivore found in the shallow waters off Arnhem Land, once hunted for its meat. Dugongs also exist on the east coast of Australia, though poor coastal management has rendered them an endangered species. This rock wall also features a possum and two agile wallabies.

SELECTED SOURCES AND FURTHER READING

Allen, J. and P. Corris (eds.), 1977: *The Journal of John Sweatman: A Nineteenth Century Surveying Voyage in North Australia and Torres Strait* (St Lucia: University of Queensland Press).

Berndt, R.M., 1951: *Kunapipi: a study of an Australian Aboriginal religious cult* (New York: International Universities Press).

— 1958: 'The Mountford Volume on Arnhem Land Art, Myth and Symbolism: A Critical Review', *Mankind* 5, 6: 249-61.

— 1970: *The Sacred Site: The Western Arnhem Land Example* (Canberra: AIAS).

Berndt, R.M. and C.H. Berndt, 1951: *Sexual behavior in Western Arnhem Land* (New York: Viking Fund).

— 1954: *Arnhem Land: Its History and its People* (Melbourne: Cheshire).

— 1970: *Man, Land and Myth in North Australia: The Gunwinggu People* (Sydney: Ure Smith).

— 1974: *The First Australians* (Sydney: Ure Smith).

— 1977: *The World of the First Australians*. 2nd ed. (Sydney: Ure Smith).

— 1989: *The Speaking Land: Myth and Story in Aboriginal Australia* (Melbourne: Penguin Books).

Brandl, E., 1972: 'Thylacine Designs in Arnhem Land Rock Paintings', *Archaeology and Physical Anthropology in Oceania*, 7: 24-30.

Bullen, M., 1991: 'An interpretation of images of women in the rock art of Northern Australia' in *Rock Art and Prehistory*, eds. P. Bahn and A. Rosenfeld (Oxford: Oxbow Monograph): 53-57.

Carroll, P.J., 1977: 'Mimi from Western Arnhem Land' in *Form in Indigenous Art*, ed. Peter J. Eco (Canberra: Australian Institute of Aboriginal Studies): 119-30.

Chaloupka, G., 1993: *Journey in time: the world's longest continuing art tradition: the 50,000-year story of the Australian Aboriginal rock art of Arnhem Land* (Chatswood: Reed Books).

Chippindale, C. and P. S. C. Tacon, 1998: 'The many ways of dating Arnhem Land rock-art, north Australia' in *The Archaeology of Rock-Art*, eds. C. Chippindale and P.S.C. Tacon (Cambridge: Cambridge University Press): 90-111.

Edwards, R., 1979: *Australian Aboriginal Art: The art of the Alligator Rivers Region, Northern Territory* (Canberra: Australian Institute of Aboriginal Studies).

Flood, J., 1983: *Archaeology of the Dreamtime: The story of prehistoric Australia and its people*, latest revised ed. 2001 (Sydney: Harper Collins).

— 1997: *Rock Art of the Dreamtime: Images of Ancient Australia* (Sydney: Angus and Robertson).

Forge, A., 1991: 'Handstencils: rock art or not art' in *Rock Art and Prehistory*, eds. P. Bahn and A. Rosenfeld (Oxford: Oxbow Monograph): 39-44.

Grove, M., 1999: *An Iconographic and Mythological Convergence: Gender Motifs in Northern Australian Aboriginal Rock Art* (Michigan: UMI Press).

Gunn, R.G., 1992: 'Bulajang — A Reappraisal of the Archaeology of an Aboriginal Religious Cult' in *State of the Art: Regional Rock Art Studies in Australia and Melanasia*, eds. J. McDonald and I.P. Haskovec, (Melbourne: Occasional Aura Publications): 174-90.

Handelsmann, Robert, 1991: 'Towards a description of Amurdak: A language of Northern Australia', Honours Thesis, University of Melbourne.

Harvey, M. 1992: 'The Gaagudju People and their Language', Ph.D thesis, University of Sydney.

Haskovec, I.P., 1992: 'Northern Running Figures of Kakadu National Park: A Study of a Regional Style' in *State of the Art: Regional Rock Art Studies in Australia and Melanasia*, eds. J. McDonald and I.P. Haskovec, (Melbourne: Occassional Aura Publications): 148-58.

Hulley, C.E., 1999: *The Rainbow Serpent* (Sydney: New Holland Publishers).

Kesteven, S., 1984: 'Linguistic considerations of land tenure in western Arnhem Land', in *Further Application of Linguistics to Australian Aboriginal Contexts*, eds. G.R. McKay and B.A. Sommer (Melbourne: Applied Linguistics Association of Australia).

Kleinert, Sylvia, Margo Neale and Robyne Bancroft (eds)., 2000: *The Oxford Companion to Aboriginal Art and Culture* (Melbourne: Oxford University Press).

Lamilami, L., 1974: *Lamilami Speaks: The Cry Went Up, A Story of the People of Goulburn Islands, North Australia* (Sydney: Ure Smith).
Leichhardt, L., 1847: *Journal of an Overland Expedition in Australia, from Moreton Bay to Port Essington, 1844-1845* (London: T. & W. Boone).
Lewis, Darrell, 1988: *The rock paintings of Arnhem Land, Australia: social, ecological and material culture change in the post-glacial period* (Oxford: British Archaeological Reports).
Lewis, J., 1922: *Fought and Won* (Adelaide: W.K. Thomas & Co.).

MacKnight, C.C.., 1976: *The Voyage to Marege: Macassan Trepangers in Northern Australia* (Melbourne: Melbourne University Press).
Masson, E.R., 1915: *An Untamed Territory: The Northern Territory of Australia* (London: Macmillan).
McCarthy, F.D., 1962: *Australian Aboriginal Rock Art*, 2nd ed. (Sydney: Trustees of the Australian Museum).
McIntosh, I.S., 1996: 'Islam and Australia's Aborigines? A Perspective from North-East Arnhem Land', *Journal of Religious History*, 20: 53-77.
Mountford, C.P. 1949: 'Exploring Stone Age Arnhem Land', *The National Geographic Magazine*, 96: 745-82.
—1956: *Records of the American-Australian Expedition to Arnhem Land, Volume 1: Art, myth and symbolism* (Melbourne: Melbourne University Press).

Nelson, D.E., G. Chaloupka, C. Chippindale, M.S. Alderson and J.R. Southon. 1995: 'Radiocarbon dates for beeswax figures in the prehistoric rock art of northern Australia', *Archaeometry* 37(1): 151-56.
Nganjmirra, Nawakadj, 1997: *Kunwinjku Spirit: Creation stories from western Arnhem Land* (Melbourne: Melbourne University Press).

Parker, A., 1997: *Images in Ochre: The Art and Craft of the Kunwinjku* (Sydney: Kangaroo Press).
Powell, A., 1996: *Far Country: A Short History of the Northern Territory*, 3rd ed. (Melbourne: Melbourne University Press).

Smith, C.E., 1991: 'Female Artists: The Unrecognised Factor in Sacred Rock Art Production' in *Rock Art and Prehistory*, eds. P. Bahn and A. Rosenfeld (Oxford: Oxbow Monograph): 45-52.
Spencer, B., 1914: *Native Tribes of the Northern Territory of Australia* (London: MacMillan and Co.).
— 1928: *Wanderings in Wild Australia* (London: MacMillan and Co.).
Spillett, P., 1982: 'Mount Permain and Mount Borradaile: The story behind the naming of two Northern Territory landmarks', *Northern Perspective*, 5, 2: 3-9.

Tacon, P.S.C., 1988: 'Contemporary Aboriginal interpretations of western Arnhem Land rock paintings', in *The inspired dream — life as art in Aboriginal Australia, ed. Margie West* (Brisbane: Queensland Art Gallery): 20-24.

— 1992: 'Somewhere over the rainbow: an ethnographic and archaeological analysis of recent rock paintings of western Arnhem Land' in *State of the Art: Regional Rock Art Studies in Australia and Melanasia*, eds. J. McDonald and I.P. Haskovec, (Melbourne: Occasional Aura Publications): 202-15.

— 1992b: "If you miss all this story, well bad luck": Rock Art and the validity of ethnographic interpretation in western Arnhem Land, Australia' in *Rock Art and Ethnography*, eds. M.J. Morwood and D.R. Hobbs (Melbourne: Australian Rock Art Association): 11-18.

— 1993: 'Regionalism in the recent rock art of western Arnhem Land, Northern Territory', *Archaeology in Oceania*, 28: 112-20.

Tacon, Paul S.C. and S. Brockwell, 1995: 'Arnhem Land prehistory in landscape, stone and paint (Transitions: Pleistocene to Holocene in Australia & Papua New Guinea)', *Antiquity*, 69, 265: 676-95.

Tacon, P.S.C., M. Wilson and C. Chippindale, 1996: 'Birth of the Rainbow Serpent in Arnhem Land rock art and oral history', *Archaeology In Oceania*, 31, 3:103-124.

Taylor, L., 1990: 'The Rainbow Serpent as Visual Metaphor in Western Arnhem Land', *Oceania*, 60: 329-44.

— 1996. *Seeing the Inside: Bark Painting in Western Arnhem Land* (New York: Oxford University Press Inc).

Welch, D.M., 1992: 'Kakadu Dreaming: Ancestral Beings and Mythology in the Rock Art of the Kakadu Region' in *State of the Art: Regional Rock Art Studies in Australia and Melanasia*, eds. J. McDonald and I.P. Haskovec (Melbourne: Occasional Aura Publications): 195-201.

White, C., 1967: 'Early Stone Axes in Arnhem Land', *Antiquity*, 41: 149-52.

GLOSSARY

Balanda: a generic term for non-Aboriginal, especially for Europeans. The term is a derivation of 'Hollander'.

Bininj: a generic term for Aboriginal people.

Bunidj: a primary clan name from the regional *gunmogurrgurr* naming system. There are Amurdak-speaking Bunidj and Gagadju-speaking Bunidj. The linguist, Mark Harvey, thinks the term Bunidj is from the Amurdak language (Harvey 1992).

Djindibi: a primary clan name from the regional *gunmogurrgurr* naming system. The Djindibi who occupied the lower Cooper Creek region spoke a dialect of Amurdak. They shared their *gunmogurrgurr* name with Gagadju speaking clans on the south Alligator River.

gunmogurrgurr: regional clan-naming system of western Arnhem Land, as it was known by the Kunwinjku. The Amurdak term is iwurrumu (Harvey 1992). The *gunmogurrgurr* is the principal system by which Aboriginal people identity themselves and others — wether they be Bunidj, Mirarr, Mandjurlngunj or Djindibi etc. Those are overarching categories, often embracing many smaller, localised clans. Clans who share a gunmogurrgurr name might be associated with quite different areas, speaking wholly different languages and possibly have limited social affiliation.

The traditional owners of the Oenpelli region, for example, were Mandjurlngunj (their *gunmogurrgurr* name). They spoke the Mengerrdji dialect. There are also Mandjurlngunj people in the upper Cooper Creek region who spoke Kunwinjku. This regional sharing of primary clan names is considered unusual, though not entirely unique, and its deeper significance and substance remains largely unknown (Kresteven, 1984; Harvey, 1992).

djang: 'sacred' or significant site with special spiritual/mythological association, often connected with Dreaming characters/events. 'In the past something happened there, and the people say that place is *djang*. It might be the earth mother or the Rainbow Snake ... Many places are like this, and people say we shouldn't go to them, we shouldn't touch anything there or something bad will happen.' (Lamilami, 1974).

kunapipi: one of the primary and more recently introduced ritual sequences of Arnhem Land, principally initiatory/revelatory rituals, centred on the First Mother and Rainbow Serpent. Kunwinjku *kunapipi* rituals were observed by Ronald Berndt at Oenpelli in 1950.

maraiin: one of the primary ritual sequences of Arnhem Land. The anthropologist, Professor Baldwin Spencer, witnessed a 'Muraian' ceremony at Oenpelli in 1912, a 'special series of sacred ceremonies ... [featuring] performances associated with certain sacred sticks and stones' (Spencer, 1914). Among the Kunwinjku, the maraiin revolves around the death of the Ancestral Being, Lumaluma 'the Giant', a lustful and avaricious character who stole women and hoarded food, for which he was speared to death by Aboriginal people. The sacred objects and clan designs of the *maraiin* were released by Lumaluma on his death.

Namorrodo: a mischievous or dangerous spirit. Namorrodo is a Kunwinjku word. Among the 'old' cultures the East Alligator River region, malignant spirits were also known as 'Indada' and 'Yunggala' (Berndt and Berndt, 1989).

rarrk, or cross-hatching: the use of cross-hatching is strongly and famously associated with the contemporary Kunwinjku bark artists. Cross-hatching is rare in rock paintings, though brilliantly evidenced in some very recent, polychrome fish paintings. Cross-hatching has also been detected in some of the oldest Rainbow Serpent paintings of the Yam period (Tacon, Wilson and Chippindale, 1996).

ubarr: one of the primary ritual sequences of Arnhem Land, focussed on the mythical 'Snake Man', Yirrbarrdbarrd. During his Dreaming travels, Yirrbarrdbarrd murdered his prospective (and reluctant) wife and mother-in-law by transforming himself into a snake and crawling into a hollow log. When the women put their hands into the log, Yirrbarrdbarrd bit and poisoned them. Yirrbarrdbarrd afterwards conferred the objects and principles of the *ubarr* ceremony to the Kangaroo Man, Nadulmi, the leader of the *ubarr* ceremony. The *ubarr* drum is the hollow log, around which the rituals revolve.

yaburdurwa: one of the primary ritual sequences of southern and central Arnhem Land, thought to have originated in the lower Roper River region. The anthropologist, A.P. Elkin, who observed and described *yaburdurwa* ceremonies on the Mainoru River (200 km south-east of Mount Borradaile) in 1948, described it as 'a ceremony for the dead', analogous (or supplementary) to the *lorrkon* burial rituals (Elkin, 1961).

A SHORT GLOSSARY OF STYLES/PHASES IN WESTERN ARNHEM LAND ROCK ART

Style/Phase	Application/Subject matter
thrown object prints	objects immersed in ochre and thrown at rock surface
grass prints ('strikings')	strands and clumps of native grass, dipped in ochre and struck against the rock surface
hand prints	hand dabbed in ochre and pressed on the rock surface (positive print)
hand stencils	hand placed against rock surface, ochre blown from mouth over the hand and surface (negative print)
boomerang stencils	boomerangs and other items placed on the rock surface, with ochre blown from the mouth
Large Naturalistic Figures	naturalistic representations of animals, especially macropods, walleroos, rock pythons, emus, echidnas and possums, some freshwater fish, long-necked turtles, freshwater crocodiles; also including extinct megafauna and carnivores like the thylacine
Dynamic Figures	mostly human figures in red ochre, expressing movement, usually in profile, often running, hunting, and depicting raised spears and boomerangs; latter variations of the style exhibit noticeably less detail and animation than earlier figures
beeswax designs	native beeswax ('sugarbag') applied in daubs to rock surface, often in a pattern or to supplement an ochre painting
Northern Running Figures	style of human figure painting categorised by Ivan Haskovec (1992), featuring fine, slender silhouettes, with flowing body-lines expressing gracile movement. The style has a relatively limited spatial distribution, endemic to the lower East Alligator River (Kakadu-Oenpelli) area, and is probably contemporaneous with the Simple, Post Dynamic and Yam figure styles
X-ray paintings	paintings of humans and animals featuring the subject's internal organs; some works clearly exhibit less interest in anatomy and more attention to 'decorative' colour and elaborate hatching. Eric Brandl, who was the first to propose a typology for local X-ray paintings, identified a sequence from early 'incipient' and 'simple' X-ray types, to 'standard' and 'complex' X-ray forms (Brandl, 1982). George Chaloupka classifies X-ray paintings as either 'descriptive' (anatomical realism) and 'decorative' (internal patterning). Paul Tacon divides them into 'early' and 'recent' phases (Tacon, 1992)

INDEX

Index